GREATER roanoke REGION

virginia

Acknowledgments

Layout, design, and production of this publication by
Platinum Publishing Company, Inc.
7 Old Solomon's Island Road
Annapolis, Maryland 21401
(410) 224-1111/(800) 783-1238

Photography © 1997 by Barry Wright.
Text © 1997 by Christina Maccherone.

Cover photo artwork by Artist Albert Paley.
Commissioned by The Arts Council of the Blue Ridge.

The information in this book has been provided to Platinum
and the Roanoke Regional Chamber of Commerce, and
therefore cannot be assumed correct or free from error.
Platinum and the Roanoke Regional Chamber of Commerce
assume no responsibility for the accuracy of information
contained herein.

1st Printing, 1997.
Printed by RR Donnelley & Sons of Roanoke, Virginia.

ISBN 1-890291-06-4

Sponsors

Access
Allstate
AmeriSuites
Carilion Health System
City of Roanoke
College of Health Sciences
Comprehensive Computer Solutions
Control Systems
Elizabeth Arden
GE Industrial Control Systems
Holiday Inn Roanoke Airport
Hollins University
The Hotel Roanoke & Conference Center
Innotech
ITT Night Vision
Kroger
Lewis-Gale Medical Center
Litton FiberCom
Mattern & Craig
Norfolk Southern
John M. Oakey, Inc.
The Orvis Company, Inc.
Plastics One, Inc.
R & B Communications
R.R. Donnelley & Sons Co.
Radford University
Roanoke College
The Roanoke Regional Chamber of Commerce
The Roanoke Times
Shenandoah Life Insurance
Southeast Rural Community
Valleydale Foods, Inc.
Virginia Tech
W.W. Boxley
Westvaco Corporation

virginia

The Greater Roanoke Region — which includes the counties of Allegheny, Bland, Botetourt, Craig, Floyd, Franklin, Giles, Montgomery, Pulaski, Roanoke, Rockbridge and Wythe, and the cities of Clifton Forge, Covington, Lexington, Salem, Radford and Roanoke — preserves the natural beauty of the countryside and presents the cultural choices of a metropolitan city.

Your Open Door ...
to technology, education & scenic beauty

Photography by Barry Wright
Text by Christina Maccherone

Wall artwork of star designed by Sharon Moody of John Brusts' Roanoke College Art Department. Sign painter: Curtis Cawford. Building renovators: Mike Warner & Jess Newbern.

Table of Contents

Foreword

This publication celebrates the wonderfully unique Region so many of us are proud to call home. It is about a Region that is dynamic and changing but, at the same time, upholds traditional values. It is a Region's business community that is successfully competing in the global economy and about an area that is noted as one of America's best places to live, work and raise a family. It is about the people – our accomplishments, our pride, our progress – who make the Region what it is today and what it will be tomorrow.

The Region's magnificent beauty, with the hills of the Blue Ridge Mountains, Smith Mountain Lake, the Shenandoah Valley and the scenic changes of four seasons, has attracted visitors and residents from around the world. The Region's strong work force, opportunities for growth and incomparable quality of life have helped businesses make the New River Valley, Roanoke Valley and the surrounding areas their location of choice. The Region's 20 colleges and universities – both public and private – provide exceptional opportunities and a way of life that cannot be found any other place.

On behalf of The Roanoke Regional Chamber of Commerce, we appreciate the support from the businesses who purchased corporate profiles to make this book possible. Now we invite you to enjoy this publication and experience the wonderful life enjoyed by the people of the Greater Roanoke Region.

John M. Stroud, CCE
President
Roanoke Regional Chamber of Commerce

The bottom line?
People feel good about living here!

an introduc

Touted as one of America's best places to live by Money magazine, the

Roanoke Valley is no longer a well-kept secret. Word is getting out.

More and more people are discovering the Greater Roanoke Region and

the area continues to garner international attention for its

unparalleled beauty and quality of life. Today, nearly 500,000 people in

12 counties and six cities are proud to call this Region home.

tion

Left: As Southwest Virginia's largest mall, Valley View offers a natural and pleasing shopping environment.

As Western Virginia's largest metropolitan area ...

the Greater Roanoke Region is a diverse society, made up of people of all ages, race and creed. Many of those who are born here typically stay, and those who discover the area usually don't want to leave. The Region is a caring and spirited community where people unite to preserve it's rich history, promote the common good and prepare for a strong future. It is a naturally beautiful place that offers panoramic views of the Blue Ridge skyline, city landscapes, mountain lakes and green space. It is a hub for commercial, cultural, medical, recreational and educational activities. In essence, the Region enjoys a dynamic synergy of breathtaking beauty and economic evolution with a clearly defined vision to shape its future.

Left: Blackburg's annual street festival, Steppin' Out attracts crafters from across the nation. Above: At the heart of the Region lies Roanoke, which presents panoramic views of city landscapes, mountains, lakes and green space. Right: Surrounded by the Blue Ridge Mountains, the Region is known for its majestic beauty and natural splendor.

Surrounded by the unmatched natural splendor ...
of the Blue Ridge Mountains, the Greater Roanoke Region offers residents and visitors an unusual mix of big city opportunities, small-town charm, carefree country living and traditional Southern hospitality.

Maintaining one of the lowest costs of living as well as one of the lowest costs of doing business in the country, the Region is not only a desirable place to live, work and play, but is one of the nation's leading growth centers.

At the heart of the Region lies Roanoke, the "Capital of the Blue Ridge," "Star City of the South" and the largest city in Virginia west of Richmond. Honored five times as an "All American City" by the National Civic League, Roanoke has won a myriad of accolades. *Kiplinger's Personal Finance Magazine* named the Region as the country's seventh healthiest place to live, and *Parenting* magazine rated the Region as one of America's 10 best places to raise a family. That's just for starters.

The FBI reports that the Region's violent crime rate is nearly 60 percent less than the nation's average, making the Region one of the safest metropolitan areas in the country.

Top: 1. The historic farmers market in Downtown Roanoke. 2. Floyd County's Pine Tavern. **Bottom:** 1. Day or night, the Roanoke Valley's beauty is breathtaking. 2. The Region's people continue to uphold the natural beauty of rural farm lands such as this Botetourt County plantation.

The Region's true appeal is rooted in its people.

It's the eclectic blend of people — young and old, natives and newcomers, males and females, workers and retirees — who live here, work here and play here that breathe life into the community and make the Region what it is today.

When the early 18th century German and Scotch-Irish settlers discovered this Southwestern countryside over 200 years ago, they lived off the land. Today, the people of the Region continue to uphold the natural beauty of its rural farm lands, rolling hills, national forests, rivers and lakes.

Virginia's oldest continuously operating open air farmers' market, located in Downtown Roanoke, stays open year-round with 60 permanent stalls to give local farmers the opportunity to sell fresh produce, flowers, herbs and homemade baked goods. Locals and tourists enjoy traveling along the 470-mile Blue Ridge Parkway, the most visited national park in the country. The Region is home to one of the world's seven natural wonders, the Natural Bridge, which George Washington surveyed, Thomas Jefferson owned and the people treasure. The Region's mountains meet the water at Smith Mountain Lake, Claytor Lake and Mountain Lake. Also sprinkled throughout the Region are such natural wonders and favorite landmarks as Dixie Caverns, the New River — which is not new at all, but is the second oldest river in the world after the Nile — and the Cascades waterfalls.

From far left: 1. The Region's people work hard and play hard any time of the year 2. Pow Wows such as this one in Salem celebrate the area's Native American heritage. 3. Lexington in Rockbridge County is home to one of the world's seven natural wonders, the Natural Bridge. 4. Virginia's oldest continuously operating open air farmers' market in Downtown Roanoke.

Bent Mountain's agricultural wealth serves the Region's many farmers' markets with a variety of fresh fruit and vegetables.

There is more than beauty here.

The Region experienced its first economic boom when the Shenandoah Valley Railroad chose Roanoke as the place to intersect its North-South rail line with the East-West Norfolk and Western Railroad. The infant industry brought new residents into the Region which quickly became a booming railroad town where life centered around the railroad, its shops and local saloons. To encourage a balance, community citizens — many of whom cherished their Irish heritage — raised approximately $100,000 from 1889 to 1902 to build Saint Andrew's Catholic Church, which stands on the original property made available through the railroad's generosity and continues to be an active parish. In 1992, a community-wide campaign raised $7 million from 2,500 individuals and 300 businesses to renovate the Hotel Roanoke, the "Grand Old Lady," with a conference center.

A crossroads community and transportation center since its railroad beginnings, the Region is conveniently located within a day's drive to two-thirds of the United States population and is within 500 miles of New York, Philadelphia, Cleveland, Washington, D.C., Nashville and Atlanta. Its central position — Troutville's exit 150 is reportedly one of the busiest exits along Interstate 81, according to the Virginia Department of Transportation — makes the Region an ideal place for many global enterprises.

From far left: 1. "The Railroad" *helped give Roanokers a start in 1881 when the Shenandoah Valley Railroad chose the former Big Lick as the place to intersect its rail line with the Norfolk and Western Railroad. 2. Saint Andrew's Catholic Church stands on the original property made available through the railroad's generosity.* **Below:** *Roanoke's central location to the rest of the country marks the area as a crossroads community.*

Its mid-Atlantic location on I-81, with access to Interstates 77 and 64, as well as a major air cargo terminal, UPS hub and a major rail system, links the Region to the world, making it a natural distribution center.

Designated officially as Virginia's Technology Corridor by the General Assembly, the Region attracts a variety of high-tech companies that rely on a skilled work force, need easy access to one of America's leading research and engineering universities, and can utilize the world's most advanced telecommunications infrastructure system to produce such modern-day technologies as wireless communications, robotics, fiber optics, magnetic bearings and night vision goggles. Innovative technologies continue emerging and more are on the horizon.

As Western Virginia's health care leader, area citizens value their accessibility to state-of-the-art medical facilities and the latest medical technology. Home to Carilion Health System — one of the Commonwealth's largest health care providers, Columbia Healthcare of Southwest Virginia – part of the world's largest health care provider, three teaching hospitals, and the Veterans Administration Medical Center, the Region provides a higher percentage of doctors per capita than most communities.

From far left: 1. The Greater Roanoke Region continues to be a transportation hub. 2. Roanoke Memorial Hospital is one of many health care facilities that make Roanoke one of America's healthiest places to live.

The Region's people also treasure
the notable educational assets.

Within a 60-mile radius, the Region boasts 20 colleges and universities, some dating to the 1840s, that produce a highly-trained work force of more than 13,000 graduates a year. That's the second highest number of college students per capita in the nation. Virginia Tech in Blacksburg was the country's first land-grant institution that has grown into the state's largest and one of the nation's most respected research universities. It provides over 1,400 of the country's most sought-after engineering graduates each year and is home to a nationally ranked college football team. In Lexington, America's first state-supported military college, Virginia Military Institute, continues preparing top-flight military officers and citizen soldiers who are, at a moment's notice, ready to defend our country. Influencing the past, present and future success of the nation's military, VMI alumni have fought and died in every major conflict since the Mexican War.

As the arts and entertainment center of Western Virginia, the Region offers the traditional "something for everyone ..."

GEORGE C. MARSHALL

V.M.I. CLASS OF 1901

… from the internationally acclaimed Center in the Square with its multi-cultural museum, Broadway-quality Mill Mountain Theatre productions and fine arts center to first-rate concerts by the highly praised Roanoke Symphony, to Virginia's only outdoor theater pageant, *The Long Way Home* in Radford.

Surprising to many, Roanoke is also a culinary mecca with more restaurants per capita than any other Virginia city.

While the Region retains its exceptional quality of life and it's citizens respect their surroundings, it also keeps it's eye on planned economic growth. In fact, Roanoke is one of the country's top 100 hot spots for business development, according to *Inc.* magazine.

The Region's forward-thinking citizens, business leaders and

government officials continue to partner together to prepare for a bright

and promising future. To help set the stage for a new era for Western

Virginia, a group of more than 1,000 volunteers from communities

throughout the Region created the New Century Council, researched

and formed a vision of where the Region is headed as it anticipates even

greater growth and positions itself as a leader in the 21st Century.

Several things are sure to happen. The Region will continue to grow. It

will maintain and build on its reputation as an educational leader. It

will strengthen its reputation as a commercial, cultural, medical and

recreational hub. The Region will emerge as one of the nation's premier

technology and development centers. And the Region will continue to be

a place where people enjoy a balanced, quality life.

A spectacular night view of the Roanoke Valley from the Mill Mountain overlook.

a rich histo

In its earliest days, buffalo, deer and elk roamed the land. Indians

lived off it. Frontiersmen explored it and the Germans and Scotch-

Irish settled it. Nestled amid the Blue Ridge Mountains, natural lakes

and rivers, the Region's rich resources offered a land of promise. The

Greater Roanoke Region's central location to the rest of the country set

the stage and marked the area as a crossroads. Native American

Indian trails and warrior paths forked here. Such early roads as the

Great Wagon Road and the Wilderness Road passed through here.

The Norfolk and Western and Shenandoah Valley Railroads

intersected here. Now, some of the nation's most-traveled U.S.

highways and interstates span the Region.

r y

Left: Roanoke's Explore Park represents the life and times of early America.

Establishing early roots of independence, such pioneers as Daniel Boone and Davy Crockett traveled through the Region, while some of America's founding fathers and government leaders knew this rich land. Two of the country's later presidents, Colonel Rutherford B. Hayes and Lieutenant William McKinley, fought a Civil War battle at Cloyd's Mountain in Pulaski County. Thomas Jefferson built a retreat home at Poplar Forest in Bedford County and owned the Natural Bridge near Lexington. His architecture work influenced the design of the original Greek-column Fincastle Courthouse, which is one of the hundreds of places throughout the Region registered with the Virginia Historic Landmarks Commission and listed on the National Register of Historic Places. George Washington surveyed the Natural Bridge near Lexington and carved his initials in the stone wall where they can still be seen today. Two Virginia governors, James Patton Preston and John Buchanan Floyd, were born at the 2000-acre Smithfield Plantation in Blacksburg, built in 1772. Now adjacent to Virginia Tech, the Smithfield House is owned by the Association for the Preservation of Virginia Antiquities.

For centuries, the Region's economy centered around agriculture. The people raised horses, cows and hogs. They planted fruit orchards. They harvested vegetables, wheat and tobacco. They made their own butter, honey and molasses.

Top: 1. Thomas Jefferson's architecture work influenced the design of many historic landmarks. 2. Thomas Jefferson's retreat home, Poplar Forest. Bottom: 1. The historic Smithfield Plantation in Blacksburg. 2. Open farmlands are part of the Region's agricultural wealth.

In 1852, the first railroad was built in Big Lick, now Roanoke City. But it wasn't until 1881, when the people of Roanoke offered approximately $10,000 cash and a promise to sell 500 acres of land to encourage the leaders of the Shenandoah Valley Railroad to create a north-south junction with Norfolk and Western Railroad's east-west route, that the Region's economy took a sharp up-turn. With the coming of the railroad, the Region began to flourish.

Residents started building the railroad's support system, including a train depot, machine, furnace and repair shops. Decades later, these same shops produced the famed Classes A, J and Y6 steam locomotives which brought industry-wide recognition to Norfolk and Western for its steam power. In 1882, the new railroad also built The Hotel Roanoke, which instantly became a community centerpiece and nucleus of the area's social and cultural life. Over the years, the hotel has offered employment opportunities to generations of citizens, provided a place where memories of weddings, dances, parties and conventions are made, and attracted such famous personalities as Richard Nixon, Amelia Earhart and Ronald Reagan.

In 1963, a partnership between Norfolk and Western and Roanoke City founded the Virginia Museum of Transportation, a key attraction that maintains the largest assortment of railroad artifacts in the Southeast. Today, the museum has evolved into one of North America's most significant transportation collections.

The railroad, enlarged over the years by a series of mergers to become Norfolk Southern Corporation in 1982, has continued to play an integral role in the Region's development. It is one of the area's largest employers and a patron to many local charities, non-profit organizations and community efforts through financial support and active employees. Norfolk Southern trains, which cover more than 21,400 miles of road in 22 states, continue to transport such commodities as automobiles, coal and grains to some of America's most important markets and by way of the Port at Hampton Roads, to the world. By acquiring a large part of the northeastern railroad, Conrail, Norfolk Southern will usher in a new era of rail service and rail-truck competition, reshape the eastern rail system and bring competition to the largest market in the Northeast for the first time in more than two decades.

In 1917, Roanoke experienced another economic boom with the opening of the American Viscose Corporation plant, an English-based firm and the South's first manufacturer of artificial fibers such as rayon. Known as the "Silk Mill," the plant became the world's largest manufacturer of synthetic silk by the 1920s and at one time employed as many as 5,500 people. The economy continued to become more diversified, notably when General Electric opened its manufacturing facility in Salem in 1956 and created 2,000 new jobs.

The creation of Smith Mountain Lake was another influential factor contributing to the Region's economic and social impact. While it started as a favorite place for weekend getaways, the lake now draws nearly 20,000 visitors each year and is home for more than 14,000 residents. It was formed after Appalachian Power Company constructed a hydroelectric dam in the early 1960s to provide most of the electrical power to Southwest Virginia and West Virginia.

A Region with strong military ties to Virginia Military Institute (established in Lexington in 1839) and Virginia Tech (established in Blacksburg in 1872 as the Preston and Olin Institute) a number of legendary heroes called this Region home.

GAINES HALL

Colonel William Preston, for example, led patriot efforts during the Revolutionary War and built the Smithfield Plantation. His family members later donated large tracts of land to Virginia Tech. Colonel William Christian, for whom Christiansburg was named, not only fought to protect Virginia but also was chairman of the committees which drafted the Fincastle Resolutions … a document which preceded the famous Declaration of Independence but enunciated some of the same concepts. General Andrew Lewis lived in Salem and guided Virginia troops against the Indians in the Battle of Point Pleasant and later in the Revolutionary War. General Thomas J. "Stonewall" Jackson taught at Virginia Military Institute, defended the South in the Civil War and became one of history's greatest military strategists. General Robert E. Lee, who led the Confederate Army in the Civil War, lived in and is buried in Lexington, served as president of Washington College, a predecessor of Washington and Lee University.

While the United States' military played an important role in the 1944 Normandy invasion, D-Day has special significance to the Region. The heroic efforts of Bedford's Company A of the 116th Infantry Regiment, which lost 23 of its 35 soldiers on D-Day, resulted in the highest per-capita loss of any town in the country.

Civil War reenactments are a vital part of preserving the Greater Roanoke Region's heritage.

Many structures remind residents and visitors ...

of the area's past with its Southern accents, and unique heritage. Roanoke's old Southwest Historic District houses 1,600 homes and buildings erected between 1880 and 1930, making it one of Virginia's largest historic districts.

The world's largest man-made 100-foot neon star, erected atop Mill Mountain and in operation since 1949, gave Roanoke its name as "The Star City." It is a symbol to area residents and is the first sight for many newcomers. Many weary land and air travelers feel a sense of homecoming when they see the star from a distance.

*Left and above: The Region offers an unusual mix of small-town charm, carefree country living, Southern hospitality and big city opportunities. **Right**: Known as "The Star City of the South," Roanoke's claim to fame is the largest man-made star in the world.*

37

A variety of other attractions also preserve the Region's Appalachian heritage. Mabry Mill, built in 1910 and still working, is owned by the National Park Service. Its location on the Blue Ridge Parkway depicts Appalachian life with demonstrations on milling, basket weaving and wood working.

Virginia's Explore Park – a unique public-private venture which blends cultural, historical and environmental features into a 1,000-acre outdoor living history museum – represents the culture of the people who inhabited the area during the 18th and 19th centuries. Explore Park was created by the people for the people. Area business leaders donated nearly $500,000 dollars to put life to the idea. Local governments endorsed it. The Virginia General Assembly funded a planning process that involved community citizens who turned the idea into reality.

*Below: The historic Mabry Mill. **Right:** Virginia's Explore Park blends a 1,000 acre outdoor living history museum.*

While past history stands still, new history continually unfolds. Today,

the Region continues carving its name in history and the people are

molding the history of tomorrow. The area's colleges and universities

are educating future generations. High-tech businesses are creating

new technologies to better the world. Famous authors, poets, artists,

actors and leaders are emerging. All of which make the Greater

Roanoke Region a wonderful place to live.

Area citizens show their respect for the Region's past and present military influence through live reenactments.

a quality ed

Education fuels the economy. It provides fundamental knowledge to

students today, prepares people for tomorrow, creates a highly-qualified

work force, enhances the productivity and competitiveness of

individuals and businesses, and, ultimately, exerts a powerful impact

on an area's quality of life. In fact, most agree that a quality

education is one of the most important assets a community offers its

citizens and is one of the keys for a bright economic future.

ucation

Left: Educational opportunities extend beyond the classroom to museums such as the Science Museum of Western Virginia in Downtown Roanoke.

The Greater Roanoke Region remains committed ...

to providing solid education to residents of all ages. Dedicated to lifelong learning, the Region extends a myriad of educational opportunities, ranging from award-winning elementary schools and high-tech magnet centers to parochial schools, business colleges and top-ranked universities for every child and adult.

The Region's public school system, comprising more than 160 schools, integrates the latest technology with the traditional basics of reading, writing and arithmetic to educate approximately 75,000 children from kindergarten through 12th grade each year.

Left: 1. A vital transportation system makes a quality education available to all students. 2. Highland Park Elementary School in Roanoke. Below: Roanoke College is one of 20 colleges and universities throughout the Greater Roanoke Region.

In today's high-tech, high-touch world, the race to keep up with technology continues at home, in business and in education. To build the knowledge base between computers and information, students throughout the Region gain hands-on computer experience in the classroom. First graders at elementary schools in Botetourt County use word processing software to write and illustrate their work, and fourth-grade social studies classes are designing travel brochures for a Virginia location of their choice to learn desktop publishing and computer graphics.

Many of the Region's schools also provide Internet access so students can ride the information highway to discover far-off countries, communicate with international students and explore global businesses. Roanoke City's James Madison Middle School, for example, requires eighth graders to create their own world wide web page. Relying on two-way video and audio capabilities, students from Christiansburg, Shawsville, Pulaski, Radford and Franklin County High Schools can take classes from any of the area high schools, Virginia Western Community College, New River Community College, or Radford University but remain at their home location by way of interactive distance learning technology. One day, every school in the Region will join this advanced communications network.

Staying on the leading edge, a number of area schools have received national honors for their long-term commitment to technology and educational excellence.

Salem City Schools' Technology Plan has been recognized as one of the Commonwealth's best by the Virginia Board of Education. Roanoke City's public school system was chosen from a pool of nearly 200 as one of two national winners of the McGraw-Hill "21st Century Technology Planning Award" for its innovative 10-year, $27 million blueprint to implement, train and maintain students, teachers and

administration on the newest technology. That same strategy also won an "Exemplary Technology Plan Award" from the Virginia Department of Education. Riner Elementary School in Montgomery County was one of six Virginia schools selected from more than 5,000 to win the "Blue Ribbon Schools Award" from the United States Department of Education for overall excellence in educational standards. In addition, Montgomery County's Focus 2006 Plan earned an honorable mention for its efforts to prepare students for the future from the American School Boards' Journal's Magna Awards panel.

The Region is also unique ...

in that parents and students have a choice of educational options. Magnet programs, sprinkled throughout the Region and offered through a number of public schools, provide a unique learning experience designed for students who want to develop specific individual talents and interests. Roanoke City, for example, presents nearly 50 distinct curricula, including performing arts, ecology, travel and tourism and aviation. Roanoke City is the first state school system that allows high school students to earn an FAA-approved pilot license. There are still more choices.

The Roanoke Valley Governor's School and Southwest Virginia's Governor's School in Pulaski County serve highly motivated secondary school students throughout the Region by emphasizing science, math, computer science and technology. Meanwhile, Roanoke Valley high school-bound students may also choose to pursue an International Baccalaureate diploma or certificate, a worldwide-recognized program which focuses on multi-cultural perspectives, requires community service projects and allows students to earn credit for admission to colleges and universities across the globe. Offered at 500 schools in 60 countries, the International Baccalaureate program is available at Salem High School, the second high school in the state to offer the option, or William Fleming High School in Roanoke City.

Above: Teachers throughout the Greater Roanoke Region educate by integrating classroom theory with practical hands-on projects.
Right: 1. Area children enjoy amenities offered by the school's variety of fine parks. 2. William Fleming's aviation curriculum is part of the Region's unique magnet school program.

Several dozen private and parochial schools throughout the Region also provide the area's youth diverse educational programs. Montessori schools allow children – from infants to elementary scholars – to learn by doing, while other non-traditional institutions such as Roanoke's Community School offers youth ages three to 18 a non-graded environment. Church-affiliated academies throughout the Region provide educational training and encourage spiritual development, while specialized schools like the Achievement Center in Roanoke exist to teach learning-disabled children.

Area colleges and universities are an integral part of life throughout the Region.

The Region is especially known for the 20 colleges and universities that are located within a 60-mile radius of the Roanoke Valley and produce a highly trained work force of more than 13,000 graduates a year.

Virginia Tech in Blacksburg is the Region's ace and is a prominent historic landmark as well as Virginia's largest and one of the nation's top 50 research universities. Virginia Tech researchers are tackling some of today's most pressing problems and creating innovations that will improve the environment, the economy and the world. Virginia Tech, now over 125-years-old, plays a major role in fueling the Region's economy being one of the Region's largest employers with nearly 5,000 people. It enrolls over 24,000 students in nearly 200 undergraduate and graduate degree programs in eight colleges, including the Virginia-Maryland Regional College of Veterinary Medicine. It graduates roughly 3,000 students each year – many of whom fall in love with the Region and stay here to work or start their own companies. With the City of Roanoke, Virginia Tech owns and promotes The Hotel Roanoke and Conference Center, which draws thousands of visitors to the Region. Virginia Tech also offers Broadway-caliber plays on campus, first-rate musical concerts and symphonies, world-renowned guest speakers and major college sports.

Right: 1. Virginia Tech is one of America's top 50 research universities. 2. The Virginia-Maryland Regional College of Veterinary Medicine.

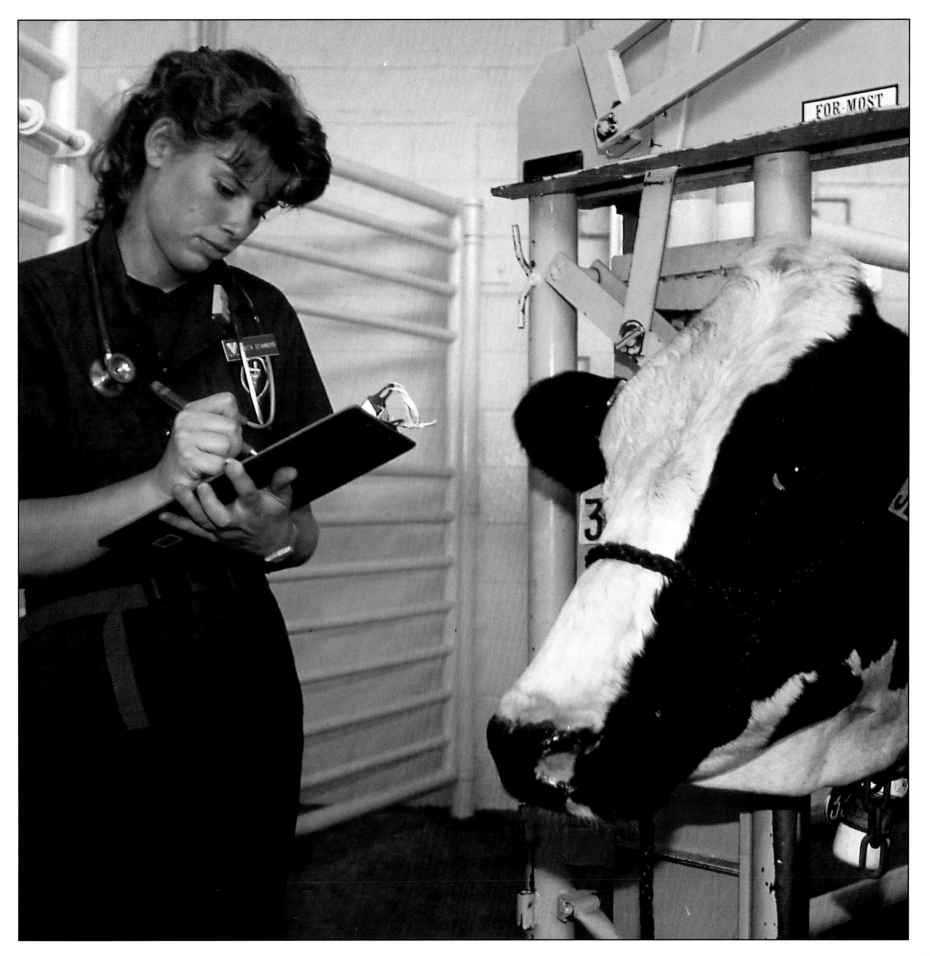

Also in its strong hand, the Region has a mixture of two and four-year; public and private; single-sex and coed; business, technical, medical, military and religious colleges, universities and schools. They include: the College of Health Sciences in Roanoke, one of the Commonwealth's largest, private health care educators; ECPI of Roanoke, a private, technical college authorized to award associate degrees in applied computer electronics technology and computer information sciences; Hollins University, Virginia's first chartered women's college that provides a career-focused liberal arts education for undergraduate women and distinctive graduate programs for men and women; Lighthouse International Foursquare Evangelism (L.I.F.E.) Bible College East in Christiansburg, a private, theological college; National Business College in Salem, the Commonwealth's oldest privately owned business college; New River Community College in Dublin, which offers the only instrumentation technology program available through the Community College System of Virginia; Radford University, which serves over 8,000 students throughout the Region by offering degree programs from its Radford campus and by partnering with Roanoke Memorial Hospital, Virginia Western Community College and the Roanoke Valley Graduate Center; Roanoke College in Salem, the nation's second oldest and Virginia's only Lutheran college, has consistently been rated as one of the top five regional liberal arts colleges in the South by *U.S News & World Report*; Virginia Military Institute in Lexington, a four-year college that combines a traditional curriculum within a framework of military discipline; Virginia Western Community College, a two-year public institution that is part of the 23-school Virginia Community College System with close to 7,000 students and offers top quality customized training for business and industry; and Washington and Lee University, the nation's sixth oldest university known for its law school.

*Above: 1. Virginia Western Community College in Roanoke is part of the 23-school Virginia Community College system. 2. Radford University. **Right:** Hollins University. Photo courtesy of Hollins University.*

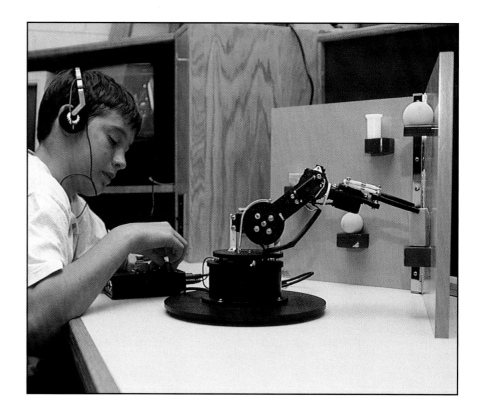

Perhaps more than any other place ...

the Greater Roanoke Region provides a strong environment for learning that is upheld by a caring and supportive community.

Area businesses, organizations and citizens share themselves and their resources with the school system each year ... as volunteers, mentors and financial contributors. The Salem Police Department began a free, week-long Drug Abuse Resistance Education camp open to students who have completed sixth through 12th grade. The program – established in 1991 as the first of its kind– has won the Webber Seavey Award for combining an educational experience with outdoor fun. A local bank donated $9,600 to the Andrew Lewis Middle School in Salem to provide tutoring for struggling students. In return, Salem teachers offer a variety of parenting classes to bank employees. Roanoke City made space available and several area colleges and universities joined forces to offer 10 master degree programs, as well as a variety of continuing education and professional, non-credit courses through the Roanoke Valley Graduate Center.

Working together, a variety of area businesses, school systems and local governments have united to make education accessible to all citizens. Many of the high schools offer training and vocational courses in the evenings for adult learners. Roanoke County Schools is Virginia's second largest adult education provider and continues to work with area businesses to provide customized in-house training programs for employees. Multiple alternative education programs are available for students with special education needs. Montgomery County's special education program received national recognition as an exemplary model for other schools to follow.

*Top: 1. Hands-on and high-tech activities such as Robotics is one of the many opportunities the Region's middle school's offer. 2. The Region's schools proceed to advance and grow with the expansion of new facilities. **Bottom:** 1. While these students learn about Audiotronics, teamwork is always encouraged. 2. Diversity continues to lend itself to the creditable education system as this student explores the realm of Aeronautics.*

To ensure an educated future for the area's educationally disadvantaged and socio-economically deprived students throughout the Roanoke Valley, a consortium of public schools and area colleges, including Roanoke City, Roanoke County and Salem public schools, Roanoke College, Hollins University and Virginia Western Community College, along with financial contributions from area businesses, civic groups and foundations, formed Partners for Students Utilizing College Campus Experiences for School Success (SUCCESS). The first educational effort of its kind in the country, the program offers financial, academic and personal support to the area's youth so that they may become knowledgeable and productive citizens.

True excellence in education requires a partnership between public and private schools, parents and instructors, businesses and governments.

A community truly dedicated to educational excellence, the Region's businesses, educators and citizens continue working together to provide knowledge to every willing person, create an environment for lifelong learning and prepare individuals and businesses for the challenges of tomorrow.

The Greater Roanoke Region provides solid education to residents of all ages.

a diverse cu

If art mimics life, then the Greater Roanoke Region is painted from a

rich palette that includes people of all ages, race and creed. The canvas

is a culturally alive area where citizens live, work and play in an

environment that conveys the feeling of small-town living and presents

the choices of an urban metropolis.

As the arts and entertainment center of Western Virginia, the Region

offers a full spectrum of musical concerts, theater performances,

historical attractions, educational museums, artistic talents,

community festivals, international eateries, churches and synagogues,

shopping venues and more.

lture

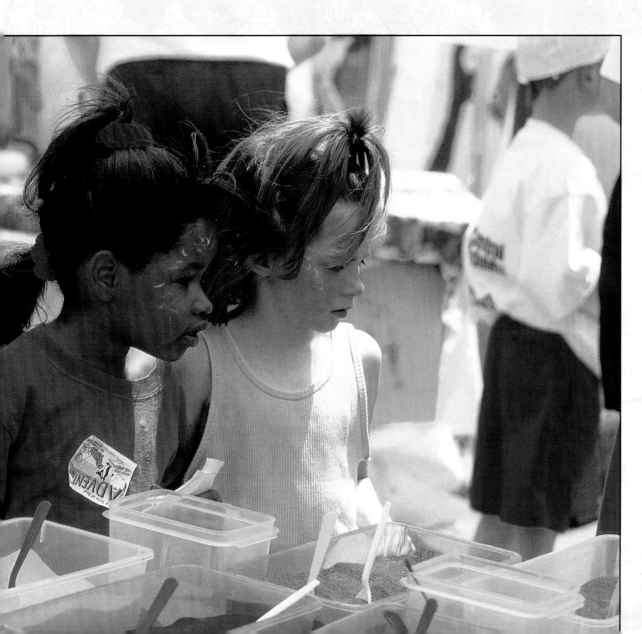

Left: Sponsoring more than 1,200 events each year, it's no wonder Roanoke was christened as "Virginia's Festival City."

Roanoke's Center in the Square ...

is the Greater Roanoke Region's cultural hub. It serves as a worldwide model of urban excellence, provides a cultural center for residents, welcomes over 400,000 visitors from across the globe through its facilities, and educates more than 100,000 children from 60 school districts throughout Virginia each year.

Top: 1. Roanoke's Center in the Square provides a multi-cultural museum and Broadway-quality Mill Mountain Theatre. 2. The Hopkins Planetarium helps visitors experience the stars and planets. Bottom: 1. Exhibit at the Art Museum of Western Virginia. 2. The Science Museum of Western Virginia's Body Tech Exhibit.

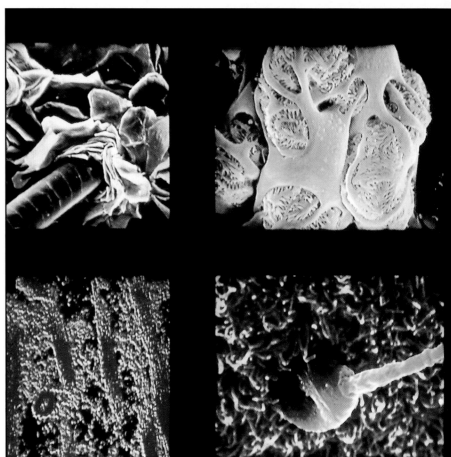

Opened in 1983 in a renovated 1914 warehouse (Roanoke's first concrete and steel building), Center in the Square is the product of a partnership between citizens, businesses, governments, private and public organizations to revive Downtown Roanoke's Historic City Market area. Today, the Center houses the Art Museum of Western Virginia, which showcases national pieces as well as focuses on southern mountain regional art and Appalachian folk art; the Science Museum of Western Virginia and Hopkins Planetarium, which offer five permanent, interactive galleries including Computers Then and Now, Science Arcade, Body Tech Exhibit, Chesapeake Bay Touch Tank, and The Rain Forest; Mill Mountain Theatre, which features two stages, world and American premieres and some of the country's finest talent; the Roanoke Valley History Museum, which traces the area's history with artifacts dating back to the 1700s; and The Arts Council of the Blue Ridge, the Region's voice for arts and culture.

Certainly unique to the Region, the Harrison Museum of African-American Culture preserves and presents regional African- American art and history, and is the only gallery of its kind in Southwest Virginia. Located in Roanoke's 1917 Harrison School, the museum is of special historic significance in that it was the first school for African Americans in Western Virginia and its principal, Lucy Addison, made her mark as Virginia's first woman principal and in fact, was the state's first African American principal. It was established by Hazel B. Thompson, the first student to attend the Harrison School. Most of the historical memorabilia and art collections for the community-based museum have been donated by area citizens and include close to 500 pieces of African-American artifacts, approximately 4,000 photographs and a large number of educational and medical relics, some from the world's first African-American lifesaving crew, begun in Roanoke in 1941.

From far left: 1. The Harrison Museum of African-American Culture is the only gallery of its kind in Southwest Virginia. 2 & 3. The Harrison Museum's collection includes nearly 500 artifacts and 4,000 photographs.

A center of activity all year long, cultural diversity abounds throughout the Region. Theater-goers can take their pick of shows. Music lovers can get an earful of their favorite sounds. Art enthusiasts can see emerging artists at work.

Regarded as one of the best regional theaters in America, Roanoke's Mill Mountain Theatre presents a full-range of Broadway-caliber shows from such blockbuster musicals as *42nd Street* and Shakespearean classics of *Romeo and Juliet* to traditional dramas like *To Kill A Mockingbird*. Established in 1964 by two New Yorkers, Mill Mountain Theatre has also presented the local talent of Nancy Ruth Patterson, a nationally-known children's book author, in its stage adaptation of *The Christmas Cup*.

Known for productions which celebrate the history and culture of Appalachia, Lexington's Lime Kiln Theatre presents nearly 100 performances throughout its May to September season, including its trademark, *Stonewall Country*, an original musical based on the life and times of Civil War hero, General Thomas J. Stonewall Jackson. Lime Kiln also features new plays by such emerging playwrights as Lexington's own Tom Ziegler, who wrote *Grace and Glorie*, which became an off-Broadway show. The theater drew its name from the 19th Century lime kiln which forms its stage and outdoor seating.

Visitors can also experience Earl Hobson Smith's famous epic, *The Long Way Home*, at the Ingles Homestead Amphitheater in Radford. Dubbed as the official historical outdoor drama of the Commonwealth, the play reveals the trials and tribulations of Mary Draper Ingles' 850-mile journey through the Western Virginia frontier.

Above & Right: Roanoke's Mill Mountain Theatre presents a full-range of Broadway-caliber shows and musicals. Left: Center in the Square in Roanoke serves as a worldwide model of urban excellence.

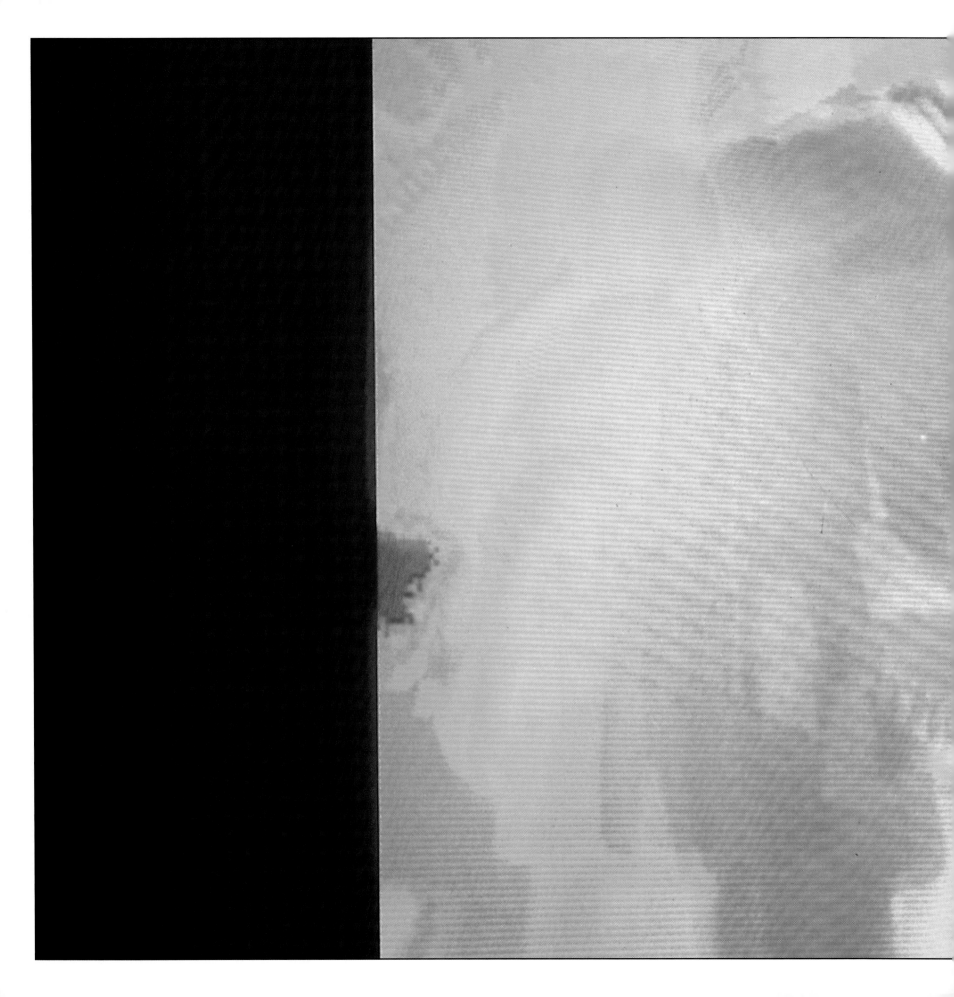

High-tech, interactive exhibits at the Science Museum of Western Virginia provide fun for the entire family.

A vibrant music scene also enriches the Region's cultural canvas.

Area civic centers, colleges and universities attract some of the best-known rock, pop and country stars. The critically acclaimed Opera Roanoke, which a small group of citizens started in 1978, has grown into the only full-professional opera in the Region with nearly 100 performers who present fully-staged productions at Mill Mountain Theatre and Roanoke College's Olin Hall. The Roanoke Symphony Orchestra performs musical offerings from classical pieces to jazz ensembles. The Roanoke Valley Choral Society, an amateur organization that involves 150 volunteer members throughout the Region, performs choral and symphonic works individually as well as in cooperation with the Roanoke Symphony Orchestra. The theater at Lime Kiln features its Coors Concert Series, where such well-known musicians as country star Allison Krauss, blues singer Leon Redbone, folk artist Mary Chapin Carpenter and legendary guitarist Leo Kottke have performed. Chateau Morrisette, Virginia's third largest winery, sponsors its Black Dog Jazz Festivals along the Blue Ridge Parkway, showcasing regional talents. The Old Fiddler's Convention in Galax draws people from all over the country and of all backgrounds every August to enjoy every music genre from country to contemporary rock songs to bluegrass.

Top: 1. Community citizens showcase their musical talents at Local Colors, an international festival. 2. Vinton's Fiddle and Banjo club prepares for an evening performance. 3. Opera Roanoke enhances the Region's vibrant music scene. Photo courtesy of Opera Roanoke. **Bottom:** *Chateau Morrisette holds its Black Dog Jazz Festivals off the Blue Ridge Parkway rain or shine.*

With more than 1,200 events each year, it's no wonder Roanoke was nicknamed "Virginia's Festival City" by former mayor and long-time Roanoker Reverend Noel Taylor. Visitors and residents alike can count on the fact that every month of the year there's always something going on – from fairs and festivals to concerts.

Far left: 1. Local talents share Appalachian folklore, song and dance. 2. Artistic , colorful displays at Roanoke's Festival in the Park. **Left**: Children throughout the Region let loose in safe environments. **Below**: 1. An Incan fire dance enchants area residents at a native American Pow Wow. 2. An annual international festival, Local Colors, in Roanoke. 3. Any time of the year, the Region's festivals offer family fun.

To promote the Region's diversity and introduce people to international cultures, Local Colors found its start in Downtown Roanoke in 1990 with four countries represented. Today, area residents from over 50 countries show their native pride at this annual springtime festival.

Among the Region's other favorite festivities are the Roanoke Valley Horse Show, the nation's only indoor, all-breed horse show that presents $250,000 in prizes; the Salem Fair, the largest free-gate fair in America and the second largest fair in Virginia with nearly 500 exhibitors and over 1,500 items, draws approximately 350,000 people; the Miss Virginia Pageant, which has been held in Roanoke every year since 1953 and is broadcast on television stations throughout America; Steppin' Out, Blacksburg's annual street festival; the Smith Mountain Lake and Mountain Lake annual wine festivals; and the Vinton Dogwood Festival that celebrates the state tree of Virginia.

Top: 1. Citizens celebrate ethnic diversity and show their native pride at Local Colors. 2. Local bands always draw crowds at Elmwood Park's amphitheater. **Bottom:** *1. The Roanoke Valley Horse Show is the nation's only indoor, all-breed horse show that presents $250,000 in prizes. 2. Blacksburg's annual Steppin Out festival offers something for everyone.*

Sponsoring more than 1,200 events each year, it's no wonder Roanoke

was christened as "Virginia's Festival City" by its former mayor and

long time Roanoke resident Reverend Noel Taylor.

While preserving the natural beauty of the countryside, the Region

presents the cultural diversity of a metropolitan city. Whatever people's

tastes for fun, art and adventure may be, the Region is sure to offer a

variety of choices to decorate their palette.

a recreation

Surrounded by the unmatched splendor of the Blue Ridge skyline,

mountain lakes and green space, the Roanoke Valley and its

contiguous cities, towns and rural areas create a recreational paradise

where variety enhances life. Virtually any time of the year, any day of

the week, anywhere in the Greater Roanoke Region, there are activities

for every age and every lifestyle.

al paradise

Left: Salem High School provides some of the best educational and recreational facilities in the state.

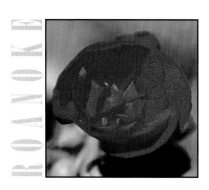

Visitors and citizens have plenty of choices.

Among them are apple picking in Botetourt County's orchards and touring historic landmarks to observing more than 130 animals, including Ruby, the Siberian tiger, at the Roanoke Mill Mountain Zoo or visiting the Zoo at the Natural Bridge. Not to mention challenging golf courses on rolling hills, horseback riding at indoor and outdoor arenas, and even spelunking in underground caves are among dozens of other recreational possibilities.

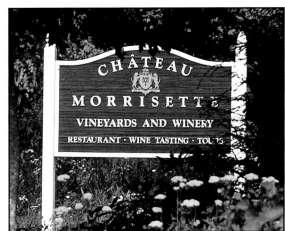

A leisurely drive along the Blue Ridge Parkway, 470 miles of majestic views, scenic overlooks and diverse attractions – from the still-operating Mabry Mill to the privately owned and regionally treasured Chateau Morrisette Winery – is a favorite pastime. Blessed with abundant forests, streams and lakes, the Region's landscape offers perfect picnic, fishing, camping and fun-in-the-sun spots where the entire family can rest and relax.

The more adventurous can consider hiking. The George Washington and Jefferson National Forests offer miles of varied terrain. The Peaks of Otter along the Blue Ridge Parkway in Bedford County provide three ranges – Sharp Top, Flat Top and Hearkening Hill – and other trails to challenge every-level athlete. A two-mile hike up to the Cascades in Giles County is well worth the effort to view a breathtaking waterfall. Or, explorers and backpackers can walk the famed Appalachian Trail, which extends more than 2,000 miles from Georgia to Maine and has nearly 220 miles of trails that run throughout the Region in Bland, Botetourt, Craig, Giles, Montgomery, Roanoke, Rockbridge and Wythe counties.

Above: Walks and nature hikes are second nature to many citizens. Photo by Sha Leigh Wright. Left: Glorious mountain sunsets remind residents of the Region's natural splendor. Right: The Blue Ridge Parkway offers hiking trails to challenge any athlete.

Those drawn to camping, fishing and hunting can lose themselves at Claytor Lake, Smith Mountain Lake and the New River Trail State Parks, which offer a full-range of land and water opportunities.

For water lovers the Region is a second heaven with several lake escapes, natural rivers and hidden creeks.

The Jewel of the Blue Ridge and Virginia's second largest body of fresh water with more than 20,000 acres and 500 miles of shoreline located along the borders of Bedford, Franklin and Pittsylvania counties, Smith Mountain Lake provides a weekend getaway for locals, attracts retirees who want to settle down in one of the country's most desirable retirement communities and lures vacationers from around the world as one of the Mid-Atlantic's most popular resort lakes. It also offers an endless array of water sports, dinner cruises and championship fishing. It is, in fact, one of the top 10 striped bass lakes in America, according to *In-Fisherman* magazine.

Pulaski County's Claytor Lake, a 4,500-acre lake with more than 100 miles of shoreline surrounded by the Appalachian Mountains, was formed when the Appalachian Power Company built a dam on the New River in 1939. Today, the lake and its state park provides a full-service marina, offers dinner cruises, fishing, boating, swimming, hiking, picnicking and camping facilities.

Mountain Lake, a 2,600-acre resort located in Giles County, is one of two natural fresh water lakes in Virginia. It is known as the filming location for the 1986 box office hit, "Dirty Dancing," and draws 20,000-25,000 overnight guests during its May to October peak season.

The New River, the second oldest river in the world, and the James River offer residents and visitors even more opportunities for whitewater rafting, kayaking, canoeing, tubing and fishing.

But the Region's beauty is not all visible from car or boat. Explorers can also visit such underground attractions as the caverns at the Natural Bridge Village near Lexington, or Dixie Caverns in Salem. According to the legend, two young boys and a dog discovered Dixie Caverns during the Civil War when the dog fell into the natural opening. The privately owned caverns, 100,000 years old, remain open 364 days a year for public tours and are known for their unique Wedding Bell Shelf formation under which a number of local weddings take place.

Each year, many localities throughout the Region host the state's Olympic-Style athletic competition, the Commonwealth Games of Virginia.

<u>The Greater Roanoke Region is also a sports hub.</u>

It boasts five professional sports teams. The Roanoke Wrath is part of the United Systems of Independent Soccer Leagues. The Roanoke Rush is one of 28 teams in the country that play National Minor League Football. The Salem Avalanche, a Class A affiliate of the Colorado Rockies plays approximately 70 home games at the $10 million, 6,000 seat, state-of-the-art Salem Memorial Baseball Stadium. The Pulaski Rangers, an Appalachian baseball league affiliate of the Texas Rangers, attracts players from across the globe. The Roanoke Express – affiliated with the National Hockey League's Calvary Flames and the American Hockey League's Saint John's Flames – plays 70 games per season against 25 teams in the East Coast Hockey League and draws more than 5,500 fans to its home games held at the Roanoke Civic Center.

Salem is the locale for such national athletic events as the NCAA Division II women's softball championship, the NCAA Division III men's basketball and baseball tournaments, and college football's Amos Alonzo Stagg Bowl. The Moyer Sports Complex in Salem includes four fields on approximately 20 acres of land, sponsors over 35 national, adult slow pitch softball tournaments annually and serves community youth and adult leagues throughout the year.

The Roanoke Valley welcomes the state's Olympic-style athletic competition, the Commonwealth Games of Virginia in which more than 7,000 athletes compete in over 35 sports. In addition, both Roanoke and Blacksburg have sponsored the Tour DuPont, America's premier bicycling event, which brought the nation's top cyclists and thousands of spectators into the Region.

Top: 1. The Region's professional soccer team, the Roanoke Wrath. 2. A baseball game with the Region's own Salem Avalanche. Bottom: 1. The Commonwealth Games of Virginia. 2. National Minor League Football, the Roanoke Rush. 3. Track and field at the Commonwealth Games of Virginia.

The Virginia Tech Hokies in Blacksburg bring ...

exciting collegiate athletics to the Greater Roanoke Region's sports scene. Virginia Tech's nationally ranked football team joined the Big East Conference in 1995, beat the University of Texas in the 1995 Sugar Bowl and played against the University of Nebraska in the 1996 Orange Bowl. Continuing its trend of excellence, the Hokies basketball team won the 1995 National Invitation Tournament and moved, along with 14 other sports, into the Atlantic 10 Conference.

One of America's fastest growing sports, auto racing is also prominent throughout the Region. From April to September fans enjoy a full spectrum of races at several area speedways, some of which are turning out top drivers who compete in the premier Winston Cup races. The Franklin County Speedway in Calloway sponsors late model, street stock, mini-stock, pure stock and rookie division races. Radford's New River Valley Speedway offers the only Winston Racing Series Division NASCAR-sanctioned, paved track within a two-hour radius and stages races in late model stock, limited sportsman, modified mini stock and pure stock divisions. The Wythe Speedway in Wytheville and the Natural Bridge Speedway in Lexington provide dirt tracks for the up-and-coming racers. Located about an hour's drive from Roanoke, the Martinsville Speedway features several top NASCAR events each year.

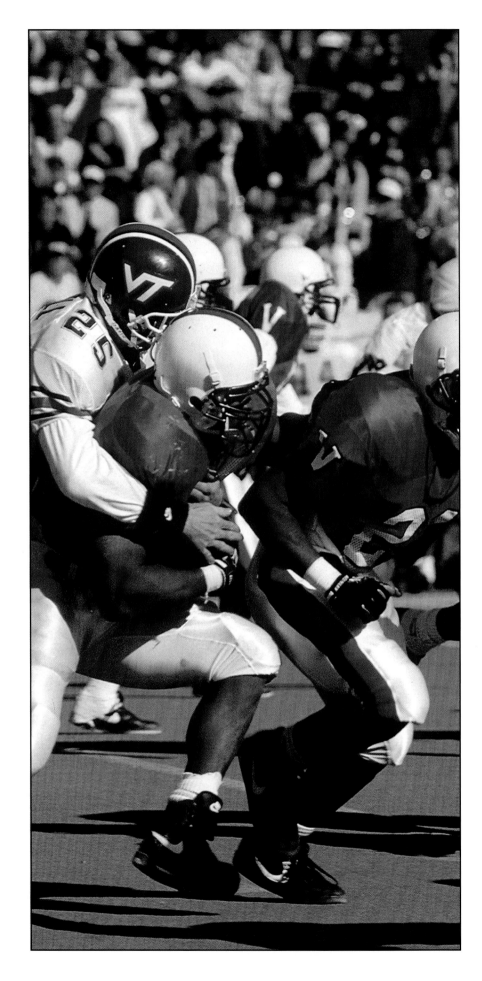

Far left: The Hokies, Virginia Tech's nationally-ranked football team. Photo by Walker Nelms. **Left and below:** Auto racing is one of America's fastest-growing sports and prominent at speedways throughout the Region such as Radford's New River Valley Speedway.

Closer to home, countless city parks, playgrounds, community tennis

courts, recreational fields, golf courses and swimming pools are part of

every town and are located in the Region's neighborhoods. Throughout

the year, individual parks and recreation departments host special

events, youth athletics, senior citizen activities, day camps, adult and

youth leagues that compete in baseball, basketball, softball, soccer,

volleyball, football, and a variety of recreational opportunities.

With all these choices, it's no wonder that the Region's people play as

hard as they work.

The River's Edge Sports Complex offers community facilities for a variety of recreational activities.

a vibrant ec

From the Industrial Age to the Information Age, the Greater

Roanoke Region's economy changes with the times, grows stronger

with each decade, and is emerging as one of the nation's premier

technology and development centers. What's more, the Roanoke Valley

and its outlying areas are blessed with a creative mix of home-grown

start-up businesses and Fortune 500 companies, a talented work force,

and some of the nation's top colleges and universities.

onomy

Left: Roanoke is one of the country's top 100 hot spots for business development.

The Greater Roanoke Region maintains ...

a well-balanced economy with a varied blend of distribution, manufacturing, service, retail, health care, professional and high-tech firms that cover virtually every industry.

One of the best places to do business in the country, the Region boasts all the qualities companies need not only to survive, but also to thrive. The Region's clean air, four-season climate, exceptional quality of life and natural surroundings help attract and maintain a loyal work force. The Region's 20 colleges and universities provide a qualified labor pool, producing more than 13,000 graduates a year and furnishing highly trained, hard-to-find, high-tech workers.

In addition, the Region's economy remains stable and rarely plunges or soars. Unlike many other places, the Region still offers available and affordable land, as well as modern shell buildings, industrial parks, corporate centers and small business incubators.

Where costs are concerned, the Region presents the best of both worlds with some of the lowest costs of living and lowest costs of doing business in the country. Overall costs, including utilities, taxes, health care, housing and transportation, are lower than the national average, but the per-capita income is higher than the national average. The result? Consumers have more money to put back into the local economy. Businesses have more money to grow and expand.

In fact, regional-based businesses continue to rank among the state's fastest-growing companies. According to a *Virginia Business* report and the Virginia Economic Development Partnership, three area firms placed in the state's top 10 employee expansion list for 1996, and eight organizations made the list of the top 50 capital investment expansions.

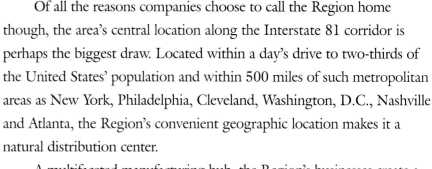

Of all the reasons companies choose to call the Region home though, the area's central location along the Interstate 81 corridor is perhaps the biggest draw. Located within a day's drive to two-thirds of the United States' population and within 500 miles of such metropolitan areas as New York, Philadelphia, Cleveland, Washington, D.C., Nashville and Atlanta, the Region's convenient geographic location makes it a natural distribution center.

A multifaceted manufacturing hub, the Region's businesses create a full spectrum of products. Some of the daily commodities emerging from the community include brand name rugs, doormats and bathroom accessories, cosmetics and fragrances, socks and athletic necessities.

The Region's companies are varied and workers make a myriad of parts for the automotive industry, which is especially drawn to the area for its prime location along the East Coast and Interstate 81 corridor.

For example, Corning Incorporated's Blacksburg plant produces ceramic substrates in catalytic converters, which help control automotive emissions, for worldwide customers. Having opened a $20 million U.S. headquarters in Botetourt County in 1997, Dynax America Corporation manufactures wet-friction clutch plates for the automobile industry, holds 60 percent of the market share in Japan and is expanding its domestic presence. Tower Automotive, the largest manufacturer of heavy truck rails in North America, makes approximately 230,000 rails per year from its $24 million, nearly 200,000-square-foot factory in Botetourt County. From its Blacksburg facility, Wolverine Gasket Division of Eagle Picher Industries manufactures roughly one million automotive gaskets a day, while Pulaski's Volvo Heavy Truck Corporation assembles more than 150,000 trucks a year.

The Greater Roanoke Region is a choice location for such manufacturers as Volvo-Heavy Truck in Pulaski.

Virginia's Technology Corridor ...

the Greater Roanoke Region is also a desirable location for high-tech companies.

The Virginia Tech Corporate Research Center is Virginia's most successful facility for moving ideas from the laboratory to the marketplace and the most successful economic development initiative, according to Opportunity Virginia, the state's strategic economic plan. In addition, it provides a home for an ever-increasing number of tenants, many of which planted their roots as a one-person business and have blossomed into national and global companies.

For example, Dominion BioSciences which began as a virtual corporation in 1993 and is breaking into the $26 billion-a-year pesticide industry with its innovative Ecologix™, an all-natural, environmentally safe birth control pill for cockroaches.

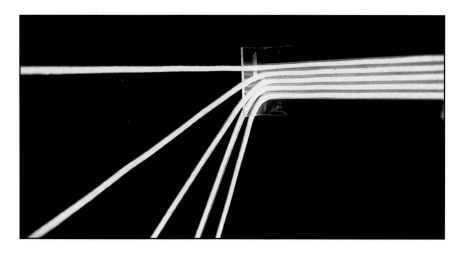

Or Interactive Design & Development, which began as an idea in 1991 and has become one of America's top 100 multimedia firms, according to *AV Video & MultiMedia Producer* magazine. VTLS Inc., the first tenant to locate in the Tech research park and the offspring of a Virginia Tech project, creates and markets library automation projects and services for more than 400 customers in over 30 countries.

In essence, small businesses drive the economy. As they succeed, grow and develop into larger businesses, they employ more people, produce more goods, provide more services and pay more taxes. As one of Virginia's leading growth centers, the Region has spawned a host of start-up businesses.

Such resources as small business development centers are scattered throughout the Region to provide free services to the entrepreneur, including business planning, marketing planning and loan procurement. The New Century Venture Center, the Region's first small business incubator located in Roanoke, offers flexible and affordable leases, shared resources and business guidance. Virginia's Division of International Trade also serves as a valuable resource for businesses interested in expanding into international markets, and Virginia's Center for Innovative Technology offers technology transfer assistance from the state's research universities and helps advise clients who are developing and marketing new technologies.

Retail presence in the Region is also strong. The Roanoke Valley

alone has more than four-million-square-feet of retail space in close

to 20 indoor shopping malls and strip malls which generate almost

$3 billion annually in sales. That's not to mention the boutiques,

antique stores, novelty shops, super-centers and discount warehouses

throughout the Region.

With a per-capita income higher than the national average and

living costs below it, all the amenities to attract and retain a talented

work force and a strong economic outlook, the Region will undoubtedly

continue to experience planned, steady growth into the 21st Century.

The Greater Roanoke Region's accessibility to transportation, health care, education and shopping

are some of the reasons it is one of the best places to live in America.

a look ahe

Already, the Greater Roanoke Region is one of the country's most

desirable places to live and work; one of the world's healthiest and

safest places to live; and a world leader in public and private

education. It is diverse, globally competitive, and one of the nation's

leading growth centers.

To prepare for planned and steady growth into the 21st Century, area

citizens, business leaders and government officials throughout the

Region continue working together to preserve its exceptional quality of

life, guard its natural environment, and enhance economic prosperity.

a d

Left: Many places such as the Blacksburg Municipal Building show their appreciation for artistic talent.

At the core of every community, though, are people.

In essence, it's the people who distinguish one place from another. It's the people who are part of the Region's highly skilled work force that helps attract and retain high quality industries. It's the people who create an entrepreneurial spirit and encourage start-up businesses. It's the people – one of the Region's greatest assets – who make things happen to shape the Region's future.

That's why more than 1,000 volunteers from communities throughout the Region helped set the stage for a new era for Western Virginia through a two-year visioning process guided by the New Century Council.

Founded in 1993 by business and community leaders, the New Century Council, including Allegheny, Bland, Botetourt, Craig, Floyd, Franklin, Giles, Montgomery, Pulaski, Roanoke and Wythe counties and the cities of Clifton Forge, Covington, Radford, Roanoke and Salem – broke new ground in an unprecedented effort in Western Virginia by encouraging the area's citizens to join together and plan their future.

Top: 1. Roanoke is a culinary mecca with more restaurants per capita than any other Virginia city. 2. A close knit and friendly community creates a relaxing atmosphere. *Bottom:* The Greater Roanoke Region is one of America's 10 best places to raise a family. 2. Area parks provide the perfect escape for rest and relaxation.

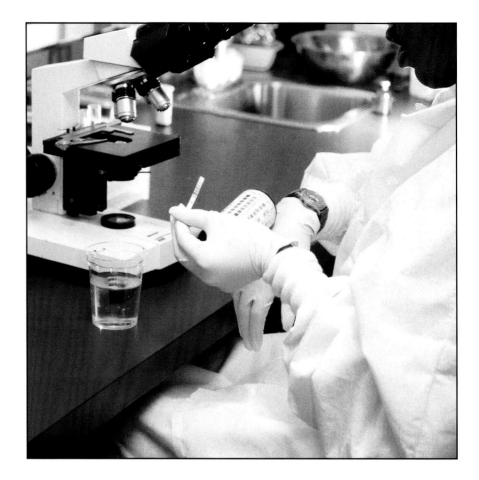

The Region will continue to grow.

In painting a picture of the Region in the next century, several things are certain to appear. It will emerge as – and is well on its way to becoming – a premier technology and development center. It will maintain and build on its reputation as an educational leader. It will strengthen its reputation as a commercial, cultural, medical and recreational hub.

Higher education and research will undoubtedly be two primary forces which will drive the future economy. While education is inherently conducive to growth, the fact that the Region's 20 colleges and universities educate more than 20 percent of Virginia's students is a cardinal competitive advantage. Together, these educational institutions will continue to produce future generations of doctors, engineers, entrepreneurs, teachers, lawyers, scientists and employees, providing the Region with a viable and highly-trained work force, and a knowledge powerhouse. The supporting function of the business community is to keep these graduates in the Region by providing new employment opportunities and high-paying jobs.

At the same time, the research originating from Virginia Tech – a world-class research university – will continue to create spin-off companies, which will, in turn, maintain and build on the Region's traditionally strong foundation of high-tech companies. These businesses will expand, give birth to new jobs and put to work the area's large talent pool.

Far left: 1. Area citizens value their accessibility to state-of-the-art medical facilities and the latest medical technology. 2. A number of businesses like Norfolk Southern have corporate headquarters throughout the Region. Left: Virginia Tech's Burruss Hall. The Greater Roanoke Region has built its reputation as an educational leader

Many areas throughout the Region continue establishing high-tech business and manufacturing parks to attract new industries.

Known for its technological strengths, the Region is home to one of the original co-inventors of fiber optic cables. It was the first place in the nation to establish an electronic village and connect an entire community, and one of the world's most prominent corporate research centers. Such leading-edge technology development centers as the Center for Transportation Research, the Virginia Power Electronics Center, the Fiber and Electro-Optics Center and the Center for Wireless Telecommunications, among others exist in the Region.

A crossroads community and transportation center since its railroad beginnings, the Region recognizes that a strong transportation network is vital to its economic well-being. It connects commerce centers throughout the nation, allows goods and products to be moved from one place to another and broadens an area's market. To this end, the Region, in cooperation with the Virginia Department of Transportation, state government and the United States Congress, is implementing several key transportation initiatives that will prepare the area for future business growth.

The "smart road" – the first Intelligent Vehicle/Highway System in the nation that is being built from the ground up – will serve as the world's model for smart engineering. It will provide a full-scale laboratory that will rely on electronic sensors, wireless and fiber optic

networks, radar and other high-tech systems to research and test the vehicle infrastructure and technologies of the future. The $103 million, six-mile, four-lane, limited access road between Blacksburg and I-81 is estimated to bring $100 million in research dollars to the Region and $300 million in high-tech spin-off companies by the year 2017. The research will allow citizens to drive "smart cars" – which will talk, determine the most direct and safest route, and automatically drive people to their requested destinations – on smart roads that will be able to determine weather conditions and report traffic accidents is being developed in the Region.

Interstate 73, which will begin above Michigan, will enter Virginia in Bluefield and will cross Blacksburg and Roanoke to run into North and South Carolina, was the vision of the Region's business community. Efforts to put the road on the national agenda were led by the Roanoke Regional Chamber of Commerce. The project, approved by the United States Congress, began in 1997 and will continue into the 21st Century to provide the Region with another major interstate. Efforts are also underway to expand the I-81 corridor from Buchanan to Christiansburg from four lanes to eight lanes to make it a safer road to transport goods and improve traffic flow.

New and existing businesses and manufacturers will ...

continue to be drawn to the area for its ability to prepare for future growth with state-of-the-art industrial parks and modern shell buildings.

For example, the Botetourt Center at Greenfield – a 900-plus acre multi-purpose park – modeled after the well-known Research Triangle Industrial Park in Raleigh-Durham, N.C., will do much more than provide a 623-acre business park to attract light and medium manufacturers. It will also offer a 133-acre planned professional office park, designate 18 acres for a new elementary school, and establish a 30-acre educational and training center that will be fully staffed by faculty members from Virginia Western Community College and Dabney S. Lancaster Community College and allow businesses to train new employees prior to an opening date. In addition the park will include a 148-acre recreation area –

complete with an equine center, horse trail around the perimeter, soccer and baseball fields, volleyball courts, an outdoor swimming pool, a community recreation center, tennis courts, picnicking areas, playgrounds and walking trails – for community citizens, as well as business tenants and their employees. The Center, a 10- to 15-year project is the first of its kind in Southwest Virginia.

In addition to the number of existing and expanding industrial parks throughout the Region, a handful of mega-industrial parks are envisioned. These will provide large tracts of land to entice additional industries.

For now and for the future, the Region will continue to uphold its reputation as a commercial, industrial, cultural, recreational, medical and educational center.

With its central location along the I-81 corridor and accessibility to two-thirds of the United States' population within a day's drive, the area will attract more businesses. With the prominent influence of the area's formidable academic community, the Region will continue to offer the cultural choices found in a major city. As a medical center for Western Virginia, the community's health care providers will continue to maintain the Region's reputation as one of America's healthiest places.

The Region is a caring and spirited community where people unite to preserve its rich history,

promote the common good and prepare for a strong future.

Although the future economy of the Region is unknown, its outlook is bright and promising. The Region's geographic location is well-positioned for new growth and its communities are well-prepared for future development. With a well-known reputation, the Region's people are supportive, optimistic and famous for making good things happen.

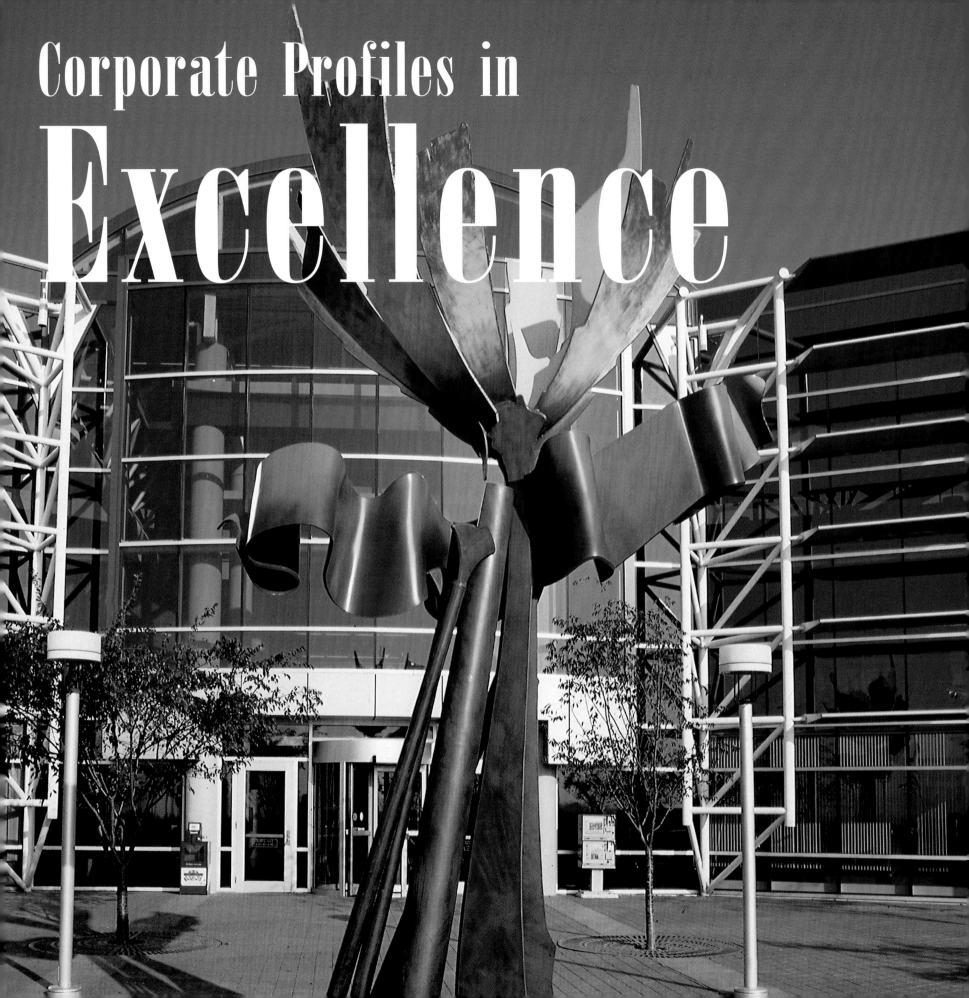

Corporate Profiles in
Excellence

Corporate Profiles in Excellence

Business, Finance & Professions

Manufacturing & Distribution

Health Care

Education

Quality of Life

Roanoke Regional Chamber of Commerce

As the Region's premiere business organization, The Roanoke Regional Chamber of Commerce is dedicated to building on the Region's many successes, facilitating steady and planned economic growth, helping existing businesses grow, and working with all levels of governments to position the Region as a leader for the 21st Century.

The Regional Chamber is one of Virginia's largest business organizations and is a catalyst for positive change. For instance, in cooperation with 12 other chambers of commerce throughout the Region, The Regional Chamber serves as one voice for over 5,000 businesses – from one-person entrepreneurial firms to internationally-known, multi-million dollar corporations. The Regional Chamber enhances the Region's quality of life by bringing the business community, local governments and educators together, by lobbying for key transportation initiatives, by promoting an exceptional business climate, and by supporting economic development through a quality infrastructure and small business development. The Regional Chamber is a recognized leader in helping existing businesses grow by sponsoring

networking opportunities, professional development seminars, exclusive member benefits, and The Regional Chamber Small Business Development Center.

Ultimately, The Regional Chamber of Commerce – guided by business leaders who serve on its visionary board of directors – provides the critical leadership necessary for the Region's businesses to compete in the new world economy. The Regional Chamber's legislative team continually works to keep the cost of doing business in the Region among the nation's lowest, while providing local and state tax revenues to local and state governments to provide quality services to businesses and citizens. The Regional Chamber has been a leader in promoting cooperation between local governments as a means of providing services to the economic Region, and with the Roanoke Valley Development Foundation, has constructed two 75,000 square foot shell buildings to attract new industries. Working with 44 other chambers of commerce in the Region, a "White House Conference for Small Business" assembled hundreds of business people to plan a national legislative strategy and is a major means of communication between the organizations that are working to promote the Region's economic prosperity.

Transportation is a key element in economic development and the Region has an exceptional transportation infrastructure. The Regional Chamber has been instrumental by promoting such important initiatives as Interstate 81 and Interstate 73. With Interstate 81 already providing an important north-south link, plans are underway to expand this important artery to eight lanes. Interstate 73, which spans from Detroit to Charleston, is now being planned with one of the first links to be positioned between Roanoke and Martinsville. The Regional Chamber has also developed a transportation plan, which is supported by local and state governments, for the Region on behalf of the New Century Council.

Existing business growth is the major economic generator of jobs in the Region and The Regional Chamber helps those businesses grow. By sponsoring networking events – including Wake Up To Business and Business After Hours – to an annual golf tournament and annual meeting to Leadership Roanoke Valley, The Regional Chamber provides ample opportunities for business people to increase their business. Publications such as Focus on Business, Valley Life, this book and The Regional Chamber's comprehensive web site (www.rrcc.org) also help promote the dynamic role of The Regional Chamber and businesses throughout the Region.

In addition, The Regional Chamber has developed a unique partnership with Virginia's Center for Innovative Technology, Virginia's International Division of the Virginia Economic Development Partnership and The Regional Chamber Small Business Development Center to offer comprehensive business assistance services – from writing a business plan and securing financing to patenting new technologies and marketing products worldwide – and to serve as an information resource for area businesses.

It was the business community that saw a need to create The Roanoke Regional Chamber of Commerce in 1890. It is the business membership that drives The Regional Chamber's efforts for positive change. It is the dedicated board of directors, business volunteers and professional staff that allows The Regional Chamber to fulfill its mission of facilitating economic growth and helping existing businesses grow year after year.

The Roanoke Regional Chamber of Commerce is – and will continue to be – a driving force that helps create a climate that is favorable for business and makes the Region the wonderful place it is to live and work.

business, finance, & professions

Allstate

Known as "The Good Hands People," Allstate is building its reputation as a great American company by providing innovative products, offering excellent service to customers as well as agents, reaching out to others through local and national campaigns, and creating a solid value for investors.

As the nation's largest publicly-held personal lines insurance company, Allstate is an industry leader. More than 48,000 employees across the globe provide around-the-clock service, peace of mind and assurance to their customers. Serving more than 28 million personal lines policies, Allstate is the second largest insurer of automobiles and homes in the United States. The company provides more than 2.9 million policies to higher-than-average risk drivers and has become the largest non-standard automobile insurance carrier in the nation. Allstate offers a diverse range of life insurance and annuity products to meet customers' changing needs, and as a result, is one of the fastest-growing life insurance companies in the industry.

In addition to its national reputation, Allstate also upholds a global presence. To stay competitive in a growing global economy,

Allstate maintains international offices in Germany, Southeast Asia, Japan and South Korea.

Regionally, Allstate is also a key player and strong economic enterprise. Drawn to the area for its strong work force, qualified labor pool and quality of life, Allstate opened its first offices in Downtown Roanoke in 1951 and has been one of the area's leading employers year after year.

Demonstrating their reputation as the Good Hands People, the Roanoke-based Allstate support center employees consistently surpass over 250 Allstate offices across the country in annual United Way donor participation. The local Allstate team also participates in such community outreach efforts as the March of Dimes, the Junior Diabetes Foundation, the Relay for Life Cancer Walk, Junior Achievement and the American Red Cross. In addition, Allstate sponsors a number of After Prom Parties for local high schools to promote automobile safety and remind area youth about the dangers of drinking and driving.

The upscale Allstate building off Route 419 in Roanoke — which has been a local landmark since 1969 — now serves as one of

two company-wide support systems. Interesting to note, the company at one time operated 22 support centers throughout the country. Emerging technologies and computer automation made it possible for Allstate to consolidate those offices into two main centers, one of which they kept in the Roanoke Valley. Local representatives at the Blue Ridge Support Center handle more than 2 million phone calls per year, support approximately 9,000 agents in 30 states, and process policies for more than 14 million customers across the United States.

Always looking to its future, Allstate believes in placing the right information in the hands of the right people and largely relies on the fastest technology to accomplish this goal. Allstate agents were among the first in the industry to use computers to process new business, produce quotes and file on-the-spot claims. Allstate operates a company-wide, integrated web-based system that allows

employees to connect faster, share information and respond to customers more efficiently than ever before. Allstate's world-wide web site at www.allstate.com provides customers direct access to the latest information about Allstate's products and services. As Allstate continues to grow and prosper, the Blue Ridge Support Center is expanding to provide 24-hour, seven days a week service to its ever-increasing customer base.

Continually seeking and building new opportunities is part of Allstate's success. As Allstate prepares for the 21st century, the company is committed to building trust by aligning actions with words; to treating people — employees and customers — with dignity and respect; to building on its longstanding reputation for customer and public service; and making being in good hands with Allstate "the only place to be."

Mattern & Craig

Established in 1978, Mattern & Craig, Consulting Engineers and Surveyors, has made a difference.

They have designed key roads, bridges, highways and interchanges throughout the Greater Roanoke Valley Region. They have also designed the infrastructure for prominent industrial parks, buildings, warehouses, community parks and recreation facilities that help make Roanoke one of the best places to live, work and play. Mattern & Craig has planned and developed sites for a wide variety of clients, including government agencies, private, institutional and commercial businesses and industries.

Maintaining corporate offices in Downtown Roanoke, as well as in Kingsport, Tennessee, and Asheville, North Carolina, Mattern & Craig offers comprehensive civil engineering services to clients, including site planning, surveying, grading, erosion control, layout plans and plats, infrastructure design, utilities, storm water management and construction administration. Their employees live throughout the Greater Roanoke Region.

The employee-owned firm promises to respond to customers' needs in a timely manner and to provide top-notch construction documents and quality, economical engineering services. Known to

go the extra mile for their clients, Mattern & Craig always assigns one of the firm's principal owners as a project manager to assure management continuity. Mattern & Craig's work consistently helps clients better serve the public and meet their personal business needs.

With experts in civil and structural engineering, transportation, surveying, site planning and utilities, it's not surprising that Mattern & Craig has planned and designed industrial sites for Tower Automotive, Arkay Packaging, Dynax Corporation, Hanover Direct and Maple Leaf, or that they have designed new infrastructure for the Roanoke Centre for Industry and Technology and Botetourt County's Vista Corporate Park and Eastpark Commerce Center. Mattern & Craig has also designed and managed civil engineering projects for such businesses as Advance Auto, BellSouth Communications, Norfolk Southern, Orvis, Roanoke Electric Steel Corporation, Carilion Roanoke Memorial Hospital and Transkrit Corporation.

In addition, Mattern & Craig's work has touched and influenced such community-oriented projects as the City of Roanoke's Carvins Cove Water Filtration Plant and the Roanoke Regional and the

Rocky Mount Wastewater Treatment Plants. They have also designed improvements to Roanoke's Elmwood Park and have enhanced the downtown areas of Bedford and Covington. They have eased the traffic flow around Hotel Roanoke with their designed improvements to Wells Avenue, Second Street and Gainsboro Road.

Sam McGhee, president and former Roanoke assistant city manager, attributes their growth and successes to a large and qualified staff of over 80 employee owners who are dedicated to meeting the customers' unique needs. Mattern & Craig has built their reputation on providing quality engineering services, providing fast results and meeting clients' budget requirements. Time and time again, company engineers have proven their ability to manage projects, to provide and implement master planning programs, to perform under the pressure of tight deadlines, and to assist clients in securing a variety of state and federal grants and loans.

Relying on the latest technology available also helps Mattern & Craig meet the ever-changing, often demanding time critical needs of their clients.

As one client puts it, "Mattern & Craig is very responsive and professional. Their willingness to listen to comments and suggestions by the project team, as well as community citizens, in an objective manner was appreciated."

Helping prepare the Region for the 21st Century, this premier civil engineering firm will continue to improve life in the Region. Their expertise is involved in extending Valley View Boulevard and in designing a new trumpet style interchange on Interstate 581 near Valley View Mall. Mattern & Craig, will – as it has since 1978 – continue to make a difference by impacting the Region's economic development initiatives, helping businesses and industries secure solid, economical engineering solutions, and improving the communities in which we live, work and play.

For more information, contact Mattern & Craig at 540-345-9342, by fax, 540-345-7691, or by email at shmcghee@mc-rke.com.

Norfolk Southern

Norfolk Southern Corporation has a long and rich history in the Roanoke Valley. "The Railroad," as it was called by its thousands of employees and the community, helped give Roanoke its start when, in 1881, the Shenandoah Valley Railroad chose the former Big Lick as the place to intersect its rail line with the Norfolk and Western Railroad. The junction became the catalyst that drove the area's economy with its train depot, locomotive and repair shops and the now famous Hotel Roanoke. The Railroad provided Roanoke's first economic boom by attracting newcomers and businesses to the Region from across the globe.

Over generations, The Railroad has enriched the city by bringing people of various backgrounds from several railroads to Roanoke during a wave of mergers. In 1959, they came from the Virginian Railway; in1964, the Wabash and the Nickel Plate and in 1982, Norfolk and Western consolidated with Southern Railway to form Norfolk Southern, "The Thoroughbred of Transportation."

Through innovation, customer focus and financial discipline, Norfolk Southern has thrived. Today, it is a critical part of a na-

tional transportation system in a worldwide economy, extending over some 21,400 miles of road in 20 states in the Southeast and Midwest and the province of Ontario, Canada. Its North American Van Lines subsidiary provides household moving and specialized freight handling services in the United States and Canada and certain motor carrier services worldwide. The Thoroughbred's Pocahontas Land subsidiary manages some 900,000 acres of coal, natural gas and timber resources in Alabama, Illinois, Kentucky, Tennessee, Virginia and West Virginia.

Norfolk Southern – with the best safety, financial and operating performance among major American railroads – is strategically positioning itself to compete in the 21st Century. It is acquiring a large part of the northeastern railroad Conrail in a transaction that will usher in a new era of rail service and rail-truck competition, reshape the eastern rail system and bring competition to the largest market in the Northeast for the first time in more than two decades. Norfolk Southern's expanded 22-state system will give it direct access to such key markets as Baltimore, Philadelphia and New York/New Jersey to allow Norfolk Southern to deliver competitive, reliable and efficient single-system service almost everywhere in the East.

Roanoke continues to be a hub for Norfolk Southern operations. The company employs some 3,100 people locally, making it one of the of the area's largest employers. Roanoke is headquarters for Norfolk Southern's marketing operations, a police communications center, major locomotive and car repair shops and serves as one of its nine transportation divisions. The Virginia Division manages daily train operations stretching from Roanoke north to Hagerstown, Md., south to Winston-Salem, N.C., east to Norfolk and west to Bristol, Va., and Bluefield, W.Va.

Norfolk Southern and its employees are helping shape the Region through their community support and public service efforts, and with donations such as The Hotel Roanoke to Virginia Tech in 1989 and the Second Street freight station to the Western Virginia Transportation Museum in 1996.

As Norfolk Southern looks to the future, it will continue to set industry safety standards, offer unmatched service, generate growth and improve productivity. By doing so, the company will honor those railroaders from the hundreds of smaller predecessor lines that are part of today's Thoroughbred system. At the same time, it will set the stage for new generations of railroaders who will carry the industry confidently through the next century.

Norfolk Southern's success in the future will stem from the constant commitment of its talented, dedicated people intent on achieving their vision to "be the safest, most customer-focused and successful transportation company in the world."

R & B Communications

In today's high-tech society, communication is critical to every company's success. In today's fast-paced world, the ability for individuals and businesses to communicate quickly, reliably and globally is more important than ever before. In today's competitive, changing marketplace communications firms must not only be able to provide accessible, affordable and flexible services, but must be able to stay on the leading edge by providing products that meet customers demands today and tomorrow.

R & B Communications is an innovative telecommunications leader that offers residents and businesses a variety of services for all their communications needs. From reliable telephone services and wireless cable television to fiber optic networks and high-speed Internet access, R & B Communications has a long standing record of giving residential and commercial customers throughout Western Virginia what they want and need.

As the holding company of a diverse telecommunications organization, R & B Communications owns and operates such

subsidiaries as R & B Telephone, R & B Network, R & B Cable, The Beeper Co., R & B Internet, R & B Telecom and Valley FiberTel. The company is headquartered in Daleville, an outlying suburb of the Roanoke Valley.

One of the oldest telephone companies in Virginia, R & B Telephone was established in 1901 and now provides services to over 10,000 residences and businesses throughout Botetourt County. A partner in the Virginia PCS Alliance — a digital wireless voice and data telephone consortium — R & B Telephone also services more than 1.5 million residents of Western Virginia. Because of the on-going deregulation of the telecommunications industry. R & B Telephone now offers local and long-distance phone services to businesses in Roanoke and Salem which is the first time area business have had a choice about their local phone service provider.

R & B Network has constructed a local fiber optic network to provide special services to high volume business users. The firm is also a partner of ValleyNet — a 525-mile fiber optic long-distance network that stretches along the Interstate 81 corridor from

Johnson City, Tennessee to Carlisle, Pennsylvania — which is used by such customers as AT&T, MCI and Sprint. Meanwhile, R & B Cable provides wireless cable television to the Roanoke Valley, offering an alternative to satellite and wireless cable services.

With paging and voice mail services continuing to be business world necessities, The Beeper Co. upholds its status as a federally licensed radio common carrier. It provides paging services throughout Virginia and the Washington, D.C., Baltimore metropolitan area, as well as across the country, and offers voice mail services to customers throughout the Roanoke Valley, the New River Valley and Lynchburg.

Staying on the leading edge of the information superhighway, R & B Internet offers reliable dial-up and dedicated access to the Internet through local phone numbers. Many businesses utilize R & B's SuperNet high-speed

(10 mbps) wireless Internet service to maintain their competitive edge. The company's R & B Telecom affiliate supports business customers by providing them with state-of-the-art telecommunications equipment and services, including Centrex, Data, Fax, PBX and Key Systems.

Showcasing all its services and products, R & B Communications operates the company's first retail location in Roanoke's Town Square Shopping Center.

Since it was established, R & B's reputation has been built on providing not only the products and services customers need, but for offering prompt and courteous service and support. As it has done for nearly 100 years, R & B Communications will continue providing innovative telecommunications services to residents and businesses across Western Virginia for years to come.

The Roanoke Times

The first issue of *The Roanoke Times* rolled off a battered, hand-powered press in a plain frame building on Second Street on Nov. 30, 1886.

Roanoke then was a rough-and-tumble railroad town, home to 6,000. In an editorial, the newborn newspaper remarked: "On the prosperity of Roanoke will depend the prosperity of this paper. It will do all in its power for the upbuilding of the city."

Today, the prosperity of *The Roanoke Times* and of the communities it serves remain as linked as ever, and the newspaper sustains an interest in the economic "upbuilding" — as well as the political and cultural life — of a region grown to encompass the Roanoke and New River Valleys.

Circulating more than 100,000 copies to a quarter-million readers daily, *The Roanoke Times* is Western Virginia's leading newspaper. Nationally, it is in the top one percent of all newspapers in terms of market penetration.

The Roanoke Times has maintained this position by seeking new and better ways to serve readers with news and information, especially about local events; by helping advertisers deliver their messages more effectively; and by

exercising community leadership — both journalistically and as a corporate citizen.

Like many modern-day newspapers, *The Roanoke Times* is the progeny of several publications. In 1909, a group headed by Junius Blair Fishburn, then the vice president of the National Exchange Bank, bought the morning *Roanoke Times* and an afternoon paper, the *Evening News*.

J.B. Fishburn had come to Big Lick (as Roanoke was first known) in 1880 as a bank cashier. He went on to become president and board chairman. His partner in the newspaper business was a brother-in-law and printer, Edward Stone, founder of Stone Printing Co.

Four years later, they bought the *Evening World* and combined it with the *Evening News* to form the *World-News*. The evening paper operated under that name for 64 years before it was merged with *The Roanoke Times* in 1977. The afternoon edition ceased publication in 1991.

For more than half a century, the Fishburn name would be stamped indelibly on Roanoke's history as well as its newspapers. He and his family gave, among other things, thousands of books to local libraries, 2,000 acres to Virginia Tech, and land for six Roanoke city parks. His son, J.P. Fishburn, ran the newspaper for a genera-

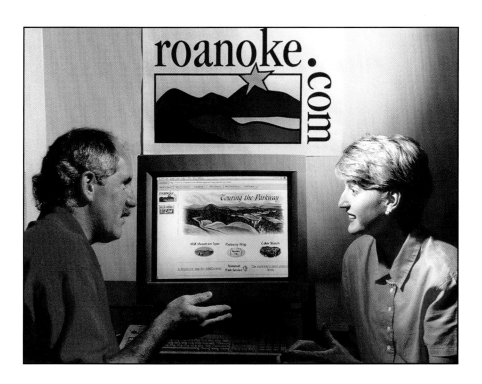

The paper won the Virginia Press Association's W.S. Copeland Award for public service four times in the 1990s, for its stories about teen pregnancy in Roanoke, the changing regional economy, and threats facing inner-city neighborhoods. Its award-winning editorial pages have consistently championed investment in children, balanced growth and regional cooperation.

Today, *The Roanoke Times* and its more than 400 employees play an active role in their communities. The newspaper is one of the Roanoke Valley's biggest corporate donors. It sponsors several special programs and events, including a yearly charitable fundraising drive. Its employees are involved in more than 50 volunteer organizations.

During the tenure of publisher and president Walter Rugaber, *The Roanoke Times* has invested in its own and the community's future. For example, work teams focus on quality improvements; an expanded press and state-of-the-art computer pagination system have been added; carriers are capable of pinpointing delivery of different products to specific households; freestanding publications such as The Daily Market Report and Homes Plus have been developed to complement the core newspaper; and a growing Internet presence — **roanoke.com** — has gained national recognition as a cutting-edge, community-building web site.

tion. He once lamented that every businessman in town knew how to run two businesses: his own and the newspaper.

In 1969, the Fishburn heirs sold the newspaper to its current owners, Landmark Communications, Inc. Based in Norfolk, Va., Landmark is a privately held company with interests in newspapers, broadcasting, cable programming, electronic publishing and specialty publications. In addition to *The Roanoke Times* and community newspapers in 11 states, Landmark owns *The Virginian-Pilot* in Norfolk and the *News & Record* in Greensboro, N.C.

Over the years, Landmark has strongly supported *The Roanoke Times'* commitment to independent, local journalism. The newspaper, in the past decade, has been a Pulitzer Prize finalist three times — for stories about abuses in Virginia communities, and life-and-death decisions in a hospital's intensive-care unit.

New technology and fast-moving market forces likely will change the way many readers receive their news and information in the future. But, in print or multimedia, *The Roanoke Times* remains committed to providing the highest quality journalism and advertising to a region whose history and growth the newspaper has shared for more than 110 years.

Access

"If you are lucky enough to find some young men with that special energy and daring which leads them into business for themselves, you will benefit from having that incalculably valuable quality serving you," said John Orr Young, founder of Young & Rubicam. "It is easy to be beguiled by acres of desks, departments, and other big agency appurtenances. What counts is the motive power of the agency, the creative potency."

Roanoke copywriter Todd Marcum and designer Tony Pearman are two such young, energetic and daring men.

In 1996 they left the security of stable jobs to start their own agency, Access. While owning a business venture is new, working together is not. Since 1992, the pair has created public service campaigns on a volunteer basis for such community efforts as the Voice of the Blue Ridge, the Roanoke Valley SPCA and child abuse prevention programs.

Working for an agency is not new either. Marcum, an award-winning writer who has received dozens of local, regional and international honors, has spent most of his career writing for

The Roanoke Times and freelancing for several local and regional advertising agencies. Pearman, who previously worked for The Maddox Agency and serves Access as CEO and creative director, has over 90 advertising awards for his work with such clients as Coca Cola Corporation, The Smithsonian Institute and United Air.

A major player in the local advertising market, Access provides a broad spectrum of advertising, design and communications services to varied customers, including healthcare providers, restaurants, retail shops and industrial manufacturers.

Their philosophy is simple. The award-winning team gives clients direct access to the people who are responsible for creating the product. The result? Streamlined communication, reduced errors and shortened design and production times, all of which saves clients' money.

Their creative potency is powerful. Access established their ability to do exceptional work, winning eight ADDY awards in the 1996 American Advertising Awards competition, the most of any agency in Southwest Virginia.

Comprehensive Computer Solutions

Keeping pace with tomorrow's technology, Comprehensive Computer Solutions (CCS) provides computing solutions, products and services to help businesses and industry across the globe take advantage of the latest technology and remain competitive. As Southwest Virginia's oldest and largest computer solutions firm, an ISO-9000 certified and award-winning company, CCS' customers include corporations, manufacturers, government agencies, public schools, universities and financial institutions throughout the region and around the world.

By providing a combination of high-tech products and a full range of computing services, CCS, established in 1981, is known for creating effective solutions to boost productivity and enhance communications. This partnering of technology with service has allowed CCS to become one of only a few Certified Microsoft Solution Providers in Virginia offering clients a full spectrum of quality networking expertise — from designing and implementing high-speed wide area networks to installing local area networks. In addition to standard networking capabilities, CCS' certified system and network engineers are able to work across multiple platforms and have, for example, connected Apple computers to IBM-compatible PCs and connected AS/400 and Unix systems to Novell and Microsoft-based networks.

As part of providing complete computer solutions, CCS offers custom applications development, industrial computer solutions and training. An authorized dealer and/or service center for a host of leading computer manufacturers including Compaq, Hewlett-Packard, IBM, Microsoft, Novell and Toshiba, CCS also boasts an extensive Service and Support Department dedicated to promptly handling all technical repairs and questions.

CCS serves such clients as Advance Auto Parts, Ericsson, First National Bank, GE, Hall Associates, Roanoke City Public Schools, the Roanoke Regional Chamber of Commerce, Snyder Hunt and Norfolk Southern.

As many computer firms have come and gone, CCS has withstood the test of time. CCS' phenomenal growth has been a direct result of their commitment not only to meet customers' needs but to exceed their expectations. By remaining at the forefront of technology, CCS will continue to serve its customers' changing computer needs. Ultimately, they will lead the way in computing technologies by preparing those customers for the new challenges of the 21st century.

For more information, call 540-382-4234 or 800-277-3077, e-mail: info@c2s.com, or visit www.c2s.com on the World Wide Web.

John M. Oakey, Inc.

In 1866, a year after the last shot of the Civil War reverberated through the hills at Appomattox, and within a hundred miles of the site where General Robert E. Lee surrendered, native Virginian John M. Oakey founded one of the South's first mortuaries.

Today, Oakey's Funeral Service is the oldest existing business in Roanoke. Still a family-owned enterprise, managed by fourth and fifth generation Oakeys, it maintains its' headquarters at the Downtown Roanoke Chapel on Church Avenue and operates chapels on Peters Creek Road and Brambleton Avenue in Roanoke, as well as Hardy Road in Vinton. In 1998, Oakey's will open a new facility on Cloverdale Road in Botetourt. Oakey's is also one of approximately 127 firms in the nation to belong to both the National Selected Morticians – where funeral homes are selected for membership – and the Order of Golden Rule, the Rolls Royce of funeral service organizations.

For more than 130 years, Oakey's Funeral Service has remained committed to meeting the needs of Roanoke Valley families by providing affordable services and products. In fact, Oakey's Funeral Service has never turned anyone away. In addi-

tion, Oakey's and its staff of more than 100 regularly help a variety of churches, civic groups and charitable organizations throughout the Roanoke Valley.

Oakey's can do as little or as much as a family desires – from conducting full service funerals to handling cremations in their new crematory – and has staff on premises available 24 hours a day, seven days a week. It also provides pre-need services for people who want to plan and/or pre-pay for their funeral arrangements to relieve the emotional and/or financial burdens that often accompany death, and operates two Options Rooms where families can select cremation products such as urns and burnable caskets.

Oakey's services don't end with the funeral. Its' friendly and professional staff promises to call on families after the funeral to make sure things are in order and that they have everything they need.

As it looks to the future, Oakey's Funeral Service plans to remain an independent operation, maintain local ownership, and promises to continue to make personal service the backbone upon which its many successes are based.

Kroger

Kroger is part of the Roanoke Valley's past, present and future.

A visionary of his time, Barney Kroger opened his first grocery store as the Great Western Tea Company in Cincinnati, Ohio, in 1883. A pioneer in food advertising, he regularly placed full-page newspaper ads and priced his goods as low or lower than his competition. A man of many firsts, his business became the nation's first food chain to operate bakeries and the first grocery store to include its own meat departments.

As a result, success came quickly.

By 1902, Kroger owned 40 stores, changed the firm's name to Kroger Grocery & Baking Company and continued to grow the business. Then in 1929, he took his first step into the foothills of the Blue Ridge Mountains, purchased almost 100 stores from the Jamison Stores Company and Piggly Wiggly, expanded into Virginia, Tennessee, West Virginia and North Carolina, located a regional headquarters in Roanoke and built a distribution center on Henry Street.

Today, Kroger is the largest supermarket chain in the United States with more than 1,300 stores throughout the country. It is also the world's largest florist.

In the Roanoke Valley and surrounding area, Kroger operates 20 stores, employs over 2,600 people and manages a 620,000 square foot distribution center in Glenvar that handles more than 935 million tons of merchandise each year. It also oversees the daily operations of its Mid-Atlantic Marketing Area – which includes more than 125 locations in six states that employ over 14,000 individuals – from its Roanoke City-based headquarters on Peter's Creek Road.

Maintaining its strong presence in the Region, Kroger and its employees regularly support the Southwest Virginia Food Bank, the American Red Cross and the United Way, as well as countless other charities and community service events. Kroger has been consistenly recognized each year by readers of the *Roanoker* magazine as the area's Best Grocery Store, and received the American Red Cross Good Neighbor Award from Elizabeth Dole in 1997 for its community contributions.

With plans for expansions under way, Kroger will continue to play an integral role in the life and times of this Region.

Shenandoah Life Insurance

A balance sheet that stacks up to the 25 largest insurance companies in the industry. A distinguished Board of Directors. Insureds numbering in the hundreds of thousands. Talented management and employees. A dynamic, professional sales force. This is Shenandoah Life Insurance Company, a vital economic presence in the Region since its founding in 1914.

Shenandoah Life provides competitive insurance products to a variety of markets: individuals and families, business owners, employers and employees and other groups.

The company is well-recognized in the insurance industry for its outstanding customer service, excellent products and superior financial performance. According to Standard Analytical Service, an independent company which bases its opinion on financial reports filed with state insurance departments, Shenandoah Life's financial performance not only stands up to, but is often better than, the 25 largest life insurance companies in the country (financial performance references investment earnings,

percentage of investment grade bonds, stock portfolio performance, solvency and net gain from operations). Shenandoah Life is rated Excellent by A.M. Best Company, while Duff & Phelps notes its "high claims paying ability."

Up-to-date technology indicates Shenandoah Life's commitment to continually provide world-class customer service. The company's computer systems conversion makes it easier and faster than ever for customers and agents to get answers to their questions and service needs. The company's web site on the Internet (www.shenlife.com) provides clients with direct, on-line access to product and service information, and opens new, expanded markets for its marketing and sales staff.

Progressive, forward-thinking management which stresses high touch service; quality, competitive products; and cutting edge marketing tools guarantee that Shenandoah Life will continue to be a viable part of the Region for decades to come.

The Hotel Roanoke & Conference Center

Nestled in Downtown Roanoke and surrounded by the Blue Ridge Mountains, The Hotel Roanoke & Conference Center is a community centerpiece.

Known as Roanoke's "Grand Old Lady," The Hotel Roanoke was built by the Norfolk and Western Railroad in 1882 to accommodate business travelers. Throughout its rich history, the luxury hotel has charmed out-of-town guests and local citizens with service, style and sophistication. It has offered traditional southern hospitality to famous celebrities of yesteryear such as Joe DiMaggio and Elvis Presley, and in more recent times, Scott Hamilton and Elizabeth Dole, as well as past presidents George Bush and Ronald Reagan. It has provided a place where residents and visitors have made memories and shared celebrations.

Today, the $42 million, newly renovated Hotel Roanoke & Conference Center retains the gracious style and elegance – from the Florentine marble floors to the vaulted ceilings – of the original, 19th century hotel. Managed by Doubletree Hotels – which operates hotels in 39 states, the District of Columbia, Mexico and the Caribbean –

The Hotel Roanoke & Conference Center features 332 deluxe guest rooms and suites, the famed Regency Dining Room and casual atmosphere of The Pine Room Pub, fitness center, outdoor swimming pool and hot tub.

While preserving its rich history, The Hotel Roanoke & Conference Center introduces the newest technology in a 63,000 square foot, state-of-the-art conference center and extends its service traditions to provide businesses and organizations with a first-class meeting facility. The Conference Center features one of the largest ballrooms between Washington, D.C. and Atlanta that can accommodate meetings for as many as 1,400 people. More than 35 meeting rooms offer Internet access and the latest multimedia, teleconferencing and video-conferencing capabilities. In addition, the center provides a personal conference consultant, an in-house audio-visual consultant and a professional staff of technicians to meet all your needs.

Listed in the National Register of Historic Places, The Hotel Roanoke & Conference Center has always been – and will always be – part of the community's soul.

manufacturing & distribution

ITT Night Vision

Most people would never expect to find the leading developer of an advanced military technology tucked away in the heart of the Blue Ridge Mountains. But that is the case with ITT Night Vision, a world leader in the production of night vision equipment for military and commercial applications. This Division of ITT Industries' Defense & Electronics group annually manufactures more Generation (Gen) III night vision devices than all of its competitors – *worldwide* – combined.

The secret behind the company's success is its ability to develop and produce – better than anyone else in the world – the Gen III image intensifier tube. An image tube is the heart of a night vision goggle. Gen III is the most advanced level of night vision technology. Via a two-stage process, the tube gathers light – present in the night sky but *not visible* to the unaided eye – and intensifies it to a level of brightness that the human eye can easily see under dark conditions. About one half the size of a D cell battery, the image intensifier tube looks plain and simple. However, with more than 400 separate process steps required to produce each tube, this critical component is *anything but simple* to manufacture.

The history of image intensification spans nearly 40 years of development. During the 60s and 70s, various technological advancements defined its progression from Gen 0 through Gen II. With each advancement, night vision devices became less bulky, lighter and

easier to use. Most importantly, their *performance* improved considerably with each generation.

By 1982, ITT Night Vision – together with the U.S. Army Night Vision Laboratory in Fort Belvoir, Va. – had pioneered the development of the most recent generation of night vision technology: Gen III. The Gen III device outperforms all of its predecessors by providing superior image intensification under extremely dark conditions.

ITT Night Vision opened in Roanoke, VA, in December, 1958 – first as the ITT Components Division; later as the Electron Tube Division – manufacturing various tubes. In April, 1973, the firm changed its name to ITT Electro-Optical Products Division (EOPD), which it retained until 1995. Later in '73, ITT EOPD began developing optical fiber and cable. The company maintained its dual product line – image tubes and fiber optics – from 1973 until 1986, when ITT Corporation sold its telecommunications business, which included fiber optics.

Since that time, the company has focused on night vision. Having been out of the fiber optics business for nearly a decade, the company, in 1995, changed its name to *ITT Night Vision* to more clearly identify the business.

The current ITT Night Vision work force of over 700 reflects diversity. Approximately 70 percent is skilled hourly labor. The balance consists of administrative, technical and professional person-

Night photography is just one of the growing applications for the image intensifier technology developed and produced at ITT Night Vision, the administrative building for which is shown here — photographed through a night vision pocketscope.

144

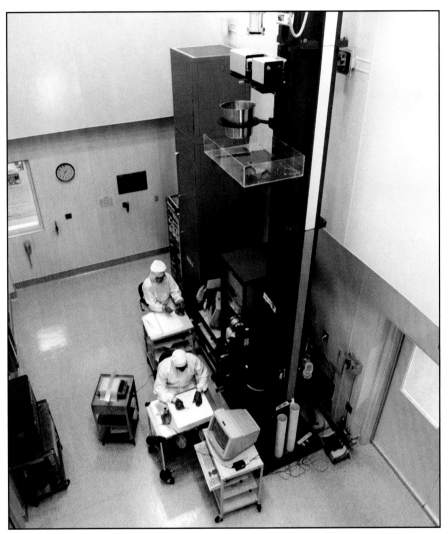

Though smaller in diameter and thickness than a quarter, the microchannel plat component consists of approximately 6 million holes — or "channels" — in which light intensification actually occurs, and its production begins in the fiber draw-tower area shown here.

– combined with product demand and employee responsiveness – has enabled ITT Night Vision to reach record-setting volumes: during the decade 1986 to 1996, ITT Night Vision produced and delivered over 250,000 Gen III image intensifier tubes throughout the world.

The majority of products ITT Night Vision has produced since the early eighties have been supplied to the U.S. Military. These include the AN/AVS-6 Aviator's Night Vision Imaging System (ANVIS), the AN/PVS-7B and 7D night vision goggles for ground forces, and the tubes required for these systems. The company has supplied 80 percent of all ANVIS, 60 percent of all AN/PVS-7B & D goggles, and 70 percent of all spare tubes procured to date. ITT Night Vision also will supply 100 percent of the new AN/PVS-14 goggles and expects to deliver over 37,000 of these systems by the year 2000.

Since 1985, the company has consistently received the *maximum allowable percentage of all U.S. Army contracts awarded for image intensified night vision devices,* reflecting the Army's confidence in ITT Night Vision to produce quality products, deliver them on time, and provide after-sale logistics support.

Another factor contributing to this confidence is ITT Night Vision's responsiveness to user feedback. Many of the design improvements and accessories associated with today's products are the result of user comments relative to form, fit and function. By listening and responding to customers, ITT Night Vision has demonstrated its concern for the safety and comfort of soldiers who fight at night.

In February, 1996, the company received 100 percent of the U.S. Army's OMNIBUS IV contract. This procurement represents the first night vision contract awarded to a single supplier since 1988, when the Army awarded ITT 100 percent of a contract for ANVIS goggles. Key to ITT's receipt of the OMNIBUS IV award was the

nel. Recruiting nationally for many of its positions, ITT Night Vision assures compensation that is competitive with high-tech industry in major cities across the U.S.

Located along Plantation Road, ITT Night Vision occupies three buildings with nearly 120,000 square feet dedicated to manufacturing.   Many processes operate around the clock. Such capacity company's development of the Gen III Ultra tube, which offers the highest performance attainable in the industry. A major factor in future procurements will be successful development of a still more advanced tube.

ITT Night Vision also has established a solid relationship with the U.S. Air Force by developing night vision equipment for fixed-wing aviation. In 1993, the USAF selected ITT Night Vision to design a new Night Vision System for use in ejection-equipped aircraft. Another key development for the Air Force is that of a miniature camera, which attaches to aviator night vision goggles, for use in night-mission training. The company is also pursuing opportunities with the U.S. Navy and Marine Corps.

Over the past few years, ITT Night Vision has significantly expanded its presence overseas. Not only has the company provided complete night vision systems to foreign allies, but it also has partnered with international night vision manufacturers by supplying its Gen III tubes for use in their systems.

Considered a critical U.S. military technology, Gen III may be exported only to NATO countries Switzerland and five others: Korea, Japan, Israel,

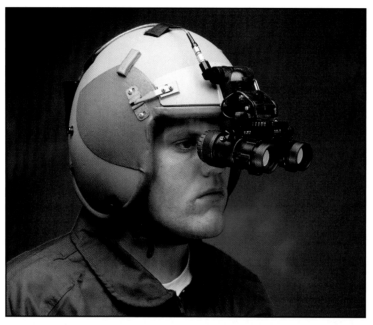

ITT Night Vision has supplied over 80% of the night vision systems used by U.S. military aviators, including the AN/AVS-9 Aviator's Night Vision Imaging System shown here.

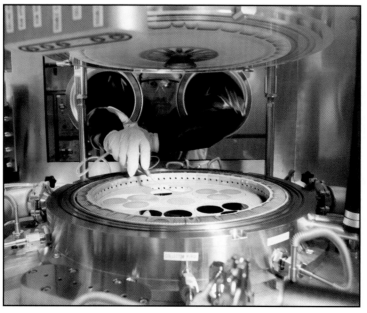

Consistent, successful manufacturing of the gallium arsenide photocathode is one of the key factors that has distinguished ITT Night Vision as the leading producer of Generation III technology.

Egypt and Australia. All other countries requesting Gen III devices must be approved by the U.S. State Department on a case-by-case basis.

In 1997 alone, ITT Night Vision captured two major international night vision contracts, both of which exceeded any international order ever before received by the company. It received a $26 million contract from Switzerland and an $86 million contract from Australia.

Receipt of these two contracts has helped establish ITT Night Vision as a dominant player in the international marketplace. Such achievement translates into good news for the community as well. The increase in business has generated a major facilities expansion for the company *and* many new jobs.

Like other defense contractors faced with military downsizing, ITT Night Vision has looked beyond its traditional military customer for new business. In addition to pursuing international markets, the company has transitioned into commercial/ consumer markets.

1993 was a landmark year for ITT Night Vision. For the first time in its history, the company launched a non-military product, the NIGHT MARINER, for boating and fishing. A year later, ITT Night Vision launched its second commercial product, the NIGHT ENFORCER, for law enforcement. Since then, the company has launched other commercial/consumer product lines, including NIGHT QUEST, a multipurpose product for consumer applications such as outdoor sporting, recreation and personal security, and NIGHT CAM, which can be adapted to 35-mm cameras and video camcorders for night photography.

Commercial fishermen as well as pleasure boaters may now experience the benefits of Generation III technology through products such as ITT's Night Mariner 160.

Of these commercial-product lines, the NIGHT ENFORCER has gained the most momentum. ITT's commitment to this market includes hands-on night vision training, whenever requested, at police and law enforcement facilities across the country. It also includes support of programs such as the SHARED VISION AWARD, a partnering effort between the ITT Industries' Night Vision Training Institute and the National Association of Town Watch. The Shared Vision Award, presented annually to two outstanding law enforcement officers, is the first nationwide program whereby citizens can reward officers who exemplify community-oriented policing.

Key to ITT Night Vision's receipt of major night vision contracts has been its ability to consistently ship products — in high volume — on time or ahead of schedule.

In 1997 the company further expanded its commercial business by introducing the NIGHT RESCUE, for volunteer search and rescue operations. Produced with good, working components from exchanged military products, NIGHT RESCUE has the same one-year warranty as other new commercial products, but is priced considerably lower. ITT Night Vision promotes the NIGHT RESCUE not only to volunteer search and rescue teams but also to civic groups, wishing to donate it.

During the same year, ITT Night Vision extended beyond the scope of hand-held products by introducing image intensified, CCTV video cameras for industrial, government and home security applications. Such high-tech surveillance can be invaluable for protecting lives, safeguarding assets, even combatting terrorism.

In addressing the needs of military and commercial customers alike, ITT Night Vision will continue to expand product applications and improve product performance. Though adopted years ago, the company's unofficial slogan is as true today as it was when first coined: *You Can Trust the Night to ITT.*

147

GE Industrial Control Systems

GE Industrial Control Systems is the world's leader in the design, manufacture, installation and servicing of motors, drives, controls and automation systems for a broad spectrum of utility, industrial and process applications.

General Electric opened its first plant in the Roanoke Valley in 1956, when it moved the Industrial Controls and Industrial Drives Departments from Schenectady, New York. It now has two plants in the Roanoke Valley. The main plant contains the Customer Training Center, system design and application engineering, Engineering Services, product service, turbine control engineering and manufacturing and drive manufacturing. The satellite plant in downtown Salem, contains the headquarters for GE Engineering Services OnSite™ Customer Service Center, and electric vehicle system manufacturing.

By combining both products and services, GE Industrial Control Systems can offer a wide range of drive, automation and automation service packages. Products generally fall into six categories – large process control systems, special process drives, standard drives, turbine controls, material handling systems and auxiliary drives.

Joint ventures with Fuji and Fanuc have enabled the company to maintain world leadership in the design and manufacture of small drives and programmable logic controllers.

GE's primary strength in the drives business is its vast application engineering expertise. Project management teams in each of the served markets provide essential know-how to companies interested in expanding or modernizing their plants or processes.

The company focuses on providing advanced technology products to satisfy the most demanding customer applications. Sophisticated control and power electronics labs in the main plant are able to draw on resources available from the GE Corporate Research and Development Center. The latest AC Drives provide more horsepower in 30 percent less space, have 80 percent fewer wires and connections and provide customers with many technical advantages that were not available previously.

The Salem plant also manufacturers and sells a wide array of industrial components. These include industrial brakes, limit switches, contrac-

diagnostic tools. GE controls are found on paper machines, winders, super calendars and coaters, as well as on fans, pumps, fan pumps and compressors.

Advanced control, drive and excitation technologies mean higher reliability and operating efficiencies for gas, steam and combined cycle turbines. Many power generation plants are retrofitting existing turbines with the new controls for greater efficiencies and higher reliability.

GE systems are also used for power generation auxiliaries such as pumps, fans, compressors, conveyors and turbine-starting systems. These applications focus on two critical needs of the power generation industry: energy efficiency and environmental management.

GE electrical controls have been an important part of the marine industry for many years. The plant provides the systems used for large dockside cranes, controls for off-shore oil well drilling rigs and for marine propulsion. Systems manufactured here in the Roanoke Valley are used to provide the propulsion for the new Disney cruise ships launched in 1997. With its commitment to quality innovation and service GE Industrial Control Systems continues to be a major employer in the Roanoke Valley.

tors, protective relays, large resistors and a varied assortment of motor controllers.

All operations are supported by a large renewal parts operation that stocks critical replacement parts for new and installed systems.

The global markets for GE systems include applications for metal rolling, metal processing, papermaking, mining, oil well drilling, marine propulsion, turbine controls, power generation and auxiliary drives. The company also serves the growing materials handling market with special conveyor belt drives and crane controls.

The GE Industrial control product line covers all areas of the metals industry from mining of the ore to the finished product.

Producers of steel and aluminum want improved product quality and mill productivity. GE's Industrial control and automation systems respond by providing the process models, high-performance regulating systems and automatic sequencing and control capabilities that improve quality and performance on metals processing lines.

GE has been the leader in drives and controls for the paper industry for over 70 years. For today's paper industry, GE provides high-performance drive systems and equipment, including programmable controllers, motors, operator interfaces, maintenance and

R.R. Donnelley & Sons Co.

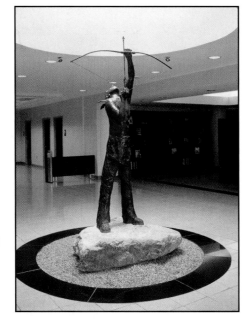

At R.R. Donnelley & Sons Company people – employees, customers and shareholders – come first.

To serve as a daily reminder of that commitment, the company's Roanoke County's Manufacturing Division – a $75 million, state-of-the-art facility with approximately 150 acres in Valley Techpark and the Region's largest economic development project in 1996 – commissioned Roanoke artist Judith Damon to sculpt a bronze, life-size Native American warrior that stands in the plant's lobby.

The statue known as Hanta Yo, which means guiding spirit, expresses the company's intentions and is full of significance. Its feet are planted firmly on the ground, practical and connected to reality. The bow and arrow are aimed at the heavens. The arrow carries within it clear intentions, the sky a place of infinite view and vision. The imagery of the warrior speaks to passion and adventure. These are the means within each of us that touch the spirit, sustain our individuality, and create the means to capture the marketplace.

Nearly a $7 billion, publicly-held company, R.R. Donnelley & Sons Company is one of the largest commercial printers in the world. It has been printing and managing information – from telephone directories to catalogs, magazines to financial documents, advertising inserts to best-selling books, including the Bible – for a diversified customer base since 1863. The Roanoke division alone produces approximately 30 million volumes of hard and soft cover, color coffee-table books such as this one and how-to-guides including cookbooks and home repair materials.

As the premiere supplier of printing services to publishers across the globe, the commercial printer is a pioneer in the development and application of new technologies. That's why it can affordably produce 2,500 to 25,000 books in a matter of days … a speed unparalleled by any other supplier, domestic or foreign. A long-time industry leader, the firm continues to stay on the cutting edge. It combines the newest technological developments to provide integrated manufacturing solutions that ensure quality and reduce cycle time. As a result, the printing giant can help customers use less paper, provide fast turn around, and produce higher quality color books.

Following through on its commitment to people, the company's Roanoke team created – and will continue developing – a positive environment for the roughly 200 individuals it employs. The roof and virtually every bay in the manu-

facturing plant has skylights. An unusually open interior, office areas do not have doors. Team rooms are available throughout the facility to give employees a convenient place where they can work together to solve problems. A large outdoor patio and indoor cafeteria provide a place where employees are encouraged to eat meals with families. And employees, at every level, are actively involved in the hiring process of newcomers.

What's more, the local division worked with area governments, local school systems and the Wildlife Habitat Council to become part of the Corporate Lands for Learning Program which is dedicated to protecting the environment. The Roanoke plant will develop walk paths for employees and will make the undeveloped land available for school children to study and explore.

Ultimately, R.R. Donnelley & Sons Company is dedicated to excellence in all that it does. That excellence is evident in the way it produces superior products for worldwide customers, creates a sense of pride among its employees, earns favorable returns on investments for its shareholders, builds strong, long-lasting relationships and respects its natural resources and environment.

Valleydale Foods, Inc.

Valleydale Foods Inc., formerly known as Valleydale Packers, has been – and continues to be – Southwest Virginia's one and only hometown meat packer.

Lorenz Neuhoff originally opened the Salem plant in 1932. An industry veteran, he grew the business each year by introducing new, quality products; by expanding into new markets; by building his loyal base of satisfied, repeat customers; and by supporting the community and its citizens.

More than 65 years later, the business is not only still around, but it still provides the preferred brand of pork-related items to households and restaurants throughout the Roanoke Valley and surrounding area.

Today Valleydale Foods' headquarters remain in Salem where the company produces its private-label brands as well as packages Reelfoot meat products. It also sells a comprehensive product line – which is made up of more than 75 Valleydale and Reelfoot brands of hotdogs, pork and smoked sausage, bacon, hams, bologna and other fresh pork items – to virtually every local grocery store and deli throughout the Greater Roanoke Region, the Commonwealth of Virginia and many states across the nation. The Valleydale brand can, in fact, be found in Northern Georgia, Eastern Kentucky, North Carolina, South Carolina, Eastern Tennessee and West Virginia, while the Reelfoot label is marketed in Arkansas, Alabama, Kentucky, Mississippi, Missouri and Tennessee. And the Salem plant alone, processes, packages and distributes more than 75 million lbs. of meat for consumers each year.

Ultimately, Valleydale Foods has built its reputation for "traditionally good" foods that are perfect for every meal – from breakfast to dinner. What's more, Valleydale's success stems from its ability to listen to consumers and give them the product variety they want. That's why Valleydale produces a 40 percent low-fat bacon and low-salt bacon, in addition to its regular bacon and brown sugar bacon. Coincidentally, bacon is one of Valleydale's largest product lines.

Business continues to grow for this hometown-based meat packer. In fact, the Neuhoff family retired and sold the business in 1992 to Gwaltney of Smithfield, Ltd., a subsidiary of Smithfield Foods Inc.

Despite the fact that Valleydale is part of a much larger company, it continues to uphold its century-old traditions and local roots. For example, Valleydale Foods and its some 400 employees regularly donate their time and/or products to such charities as United Way, the Commonwealth Games of Virginia, the Easter Seals Foundation as well as many others.

And like it has done for so many years, Valleydale Foods will continue to grow. Its products will continue to be around for many years to come. It is, after all, part of the fifth largest (a figure that is steadily climbing) meat packer in the world.

W.W. Boxley

Few companies reach the fourth generation of family ownership and management. Few businesses survive more than a century of economic ups and downs. Few firms consistently provide customers with *quality from the ground up*.

Since it was established in 1892, the W.W. Boxley Company has promised and delivered customers quality, honesty and fairness. Those values remain the hallmark of the Roanoke-based firm which is a customer directed supplier of quality construction materials including crushed stone, sand, ready-mix concrete and concrete block. Committed to honest, personal attention to its customers' needs, the team-based and customer-focused organization also owns and operates a truck fleet to deliver its materials for clients.

Relying on many long-term and qualified employees, more than a century of experience, state-of-the-art equipment and the latest environmentally-friendly technologies, W.W. Boxley's quality materials provide a solid foundation for buildings, roads, bridges and schools throughout the Region. In fact, the company's crushed stone, sand and concrete are part of such regional landmarks as the Roanoke Regional Airport, the Homestead, the Blue Ridge Parkway, Roanoke Memorial Hospital and the Smith Mountain Lake dam.

The company continues expanding by doing a good job for customers, attracting new clients and acquiring competitive firms. It operates seven quarry locations in Blue Ridge, Concord, Lynchburg, Piney River, Stuarts Draft, Martinsville and Lewisburg, W.Va., three ready-mix concrete plants in Martinsville, Oak Hill, and Summersville, W.Va. and maintains its corporate headquarters in the Boxley Building on Jefferson Street in downtown Roanoke.

Dedicated to supporting the 40 communities it serves throughout Virginia, West Virginia and North Carolina, W.W. Boxley and its employees remain active with such efforts as volunteer rescue squads, Adopt-A-School and Adopt-A-Highway programs, United Way campaigns and numerous charities. In addition, the firm supports a variety of special projects, and helped build a five-acre ballfield in Botetourt County and a Roanoke playground.

Having seen the company from the days of the pick and shovel to the high-tech, environmentally aware 90s, W.W. Boxley looks forward to the 21st Century when it will continue to provide customers with superior products, attentive service, community commitment and ultimately, *quality from the ground up*.

Elizabeth Arden

Elizabeth Arden combines tradition with technology, elegance with innovation. Elizabeth Arden maintains a local presence in the Roanoke Valley where it operates one of two logistics centers and its North American manufacturing facility, as well as a global presence as one of the top four prestige cosmetics and fragrance firms in the world. Elizabeth Arden continues to lead the $21 billion industry by creating new products, relying on the latest technology, providing superior customer service and positioning itself for the next century.

The almost $1 billion company – which distributes its cosmetics and fragrances in more than 100 countries – strategically relocated its manufacturing plant and logistics center from New York City to the Roanoke Valley to take advantage of the area's central location, excellent quality of life, educated and loyal workforce, and accessibility to a strong academic community.

The 365,000 square foot Elizabeth Arden North American manufacturing facility located on Plantation Road in Roanoke, operates around-the-clock five days a week to produce almost 12 million lipsticks, over four million pounds of creams and lotions, nearly two million ceramides and approximately 12 million specialty, gift

sets each year. Dedicated to quality control, Elizabeth Arden uses global sources for its raw ingredients, matches batch colors and does not test its products on animals.

Meanwhile, the 258,000 square foot logistics center, located in the Roanoke Centre for Industry and Technology, processes as many as 10,000 worldwide orders each day, handles customer service issues and ships over 4,000 products to more than 10,000 destinations in the United States, Canada, Puerto Rico, the Caribbean, Asia Pacific Region and Europe. Dedicated to technology and featured in a cover story by *Modern Materials Handling* magazine, the logistics center has completed $7 million in capital and systems improvements. As a direct result of automating most of its operations, the Roanoke-based logistics center has become the industry's lowest-cost provider, employs a new breed of high-tech distribution specialists and provides quick response capabilities.

As it has for almost nine decades, the Elizabeth Arden name will continue to be known throughout the world. And ultimately, the two Roanoke facilities play an integral role in that success.

Innotech

It began as one man's idea in 1988. It became a start-up company in 1990. It commercialized the first product of its kind in a $14 billion-plus industry in 1993, went public on the NASDAQ stock exchange in 1996, and was acquired by Johnson & Johnson – the world's largest, most comprehensive manufacturer of health care products and the winner of the 1996 National Medal of Technology – in 1997.

A breathtaking success story, Innotech now delivers optical excellence for less across the globe.

Innotech's claim to fame began with its creation of The Excalibur Lens System, the first major innovation in the way spectacle lenses are made since the late 1800s. The user-friendly, computer-based, desk-top size machine produces high quality, cost-effective lenses at eye care practitioners' offices in less than 30 minutes. Compare that to the traditional channels of distribution which take several days, hours of labor and lots of expensive equipment and Innotech's competitive advantages quickly become apparent ... for both eye care professionals and consumers.

Although the company got its start as a manufacturer of lens equipment, today Innotech not only produces and sells its state-of-the-

art Excalibur Lens System, but it also provides all the consumable materials required by the system, as well as offers a wide selection of specialty lens products, including progressives or no-line bifocals, high index or ultra thin lenses, and photochromics, which transition from indoor spectacles to outdoor sunglasses.

Not surprisingly, Innotech's high-quality, affordable products are available in the United States and more than 20 countries around the world. A technological front-runner, Innotech also owns nearly 20 patents and has over 60 applications pending.

Known as the world's leader for the manufacturing and sale of in-office spectacle lens fabrication equipment, Innotech operates its headquarters as well as a manufacturing plant from its original home of Roanoke, and runs another manufacturing facility in Petersburg.

A young, vibrant, leading-edge firm, Innotech, as a part of the Johnson & Johnson Vision Products Group, will undoubtedly continue to create new technologies that will increase the quality of spectacle lenses, make the jobs of eye care professionals easier, and ultimately enhance people's ability to see for a lifetime.

Litton FiberCom

The Information Technology Age is here to stay and FiberCom®, a division of Litton in Roanoke, is making a difference.

A worldwide leader, FiberCom provides high-tech multimedia access networking capabilities and products to help businesses across the globe take advantage of the latest technology and position themselves in today's global marketplace. With a history of selling high quality, reliable Ethernet and fiber optic networking products, FiberCom's customers include financial institutions, universities, media companies, manufacturers, resellers and prime contractors throughout the United States, Australia, Canada, Egypt, Finland and Korea.

Dedicated to meeting customers' multimedia access needs for high quality, reliable voice, data and video applications, FiberCom's growing business also provides Asynchronous Transfer Mode (ATM) technology to commercial and international market customers. A leading edge technology, ATM replaces T1 transmission service which has been the standard for 40 years. Now, more than ever, electronic multimedia users need high-speed transmission facilities at reasonable service rates. That's why FiberCom's ATM network access products provide transmission on demand and allow customers to pay for actual usage.

Keeping an eye to the future, FiberCom is also designing high quality video solutions for tomorrow, as well as creating new technologies. Technologies for business and residential customers who will continue relying on the Internet and all it offers. Technologies for access providers who will eventually all use ATM technology as the backbone for transmission. Technologies for businesses that will face the challenge of expanding network access to accommodate the growing number of employees who work from home. Technologies for educational institutions that will continue to offer students alternative methods of study and distance learning opportunities which will demand increased video usage.

Explosive growth is on the horizon. And FiberCom will be ready...with high-quality, low-cost multimedia access networking products to meet customers' changing needs.

Plastics One, Inc.

From the markets they serve to the way they conduct business, communication defines the heart and purpose of Plastics One, Inc. It drives who they are as a family-owned, employee-oriented company and determines superior quality and reliability to all their products.

Founded in 1949 by native Roanokers Curtis and Charles Lemon, Plastics One – formerly known as Plastic Products Company – was formed to meet the needs of the hearing impaired by supplying hearing and receiver cords and accessories.

Plastics One now serves a diverse market of domestic and international customers. 3M, GE, ITT and Hamilton Beach-Proctor Silex, to name a few in such industries as telecommunications, electronics, medical and dental. From its 60,000 square foot 20-acre manufacturing facility, Plastics One specializes in custom injection molding with engineering polymers, provides miniature precision cable and connector systems which include over 1,000 styles of connectors, receptacles and jacks, and offers pre-clinical testing components such as electrode and cannula systems. Their products meet a wide variety of needs – from monitoring the status of hospitalized patients and the health of space shuttle astronauts to bringing the beauty of sound to the hearing impaired. Research and design engineers and an in-house tool shop compliment and strengthen their expertise in custom design manufacturing.

"Since we opened our doors, our company has been based on providing what people need," says CEO and co-founder Charles Lemon. "We couldn't do that without quality people. It's our people who make the difference and it's our people who are willing to go the extra mile."

Westvaco Corporation

In the midst of Virginia's mountains lies a gem: Westvaco Corporation's Alleghany Highlands operations.

With 14,000 employees worldwide, Westvaco manufactures high-quality papers, packaging and specialty chemicals. Its Virginia operations play a key role in defining the company as a global market leader.

Covington's Bleached Board Division facility is one of the world's largest and most technologically advanced bleached paperboard mills. It stretches 1.5 miles along the Jackson River, employs about 1,500 people and produces over 2,500 tons of paperboard daily. The Division exports to more than 70 countries, where customers rely upon Westvaco's paperboard for packaging applications that preserve, protect and promote products including soaps, frozen dinners, medicines, personal care products and aseptic juices. Book covers, greeting cards and sports cards — applications that demand vivid graphics and durability — are among other common uses for Westvaco's paperboard.

Covington is also home to Westvaco's Carbon Department headquarters. A major unit of the company's Chemical Division, the Carbon Department manufactures activated carbon for use in environmental control applications and industrial purification processes.

Production facilities in Covington and Wickliffe, Kentucky supply a major world share of carbon used to clean automotive emissions.

Scientists and support personnel at the Covington Research Center focus on research and development for papermaking, converting and new products.

At the nearby Low Moor Converting and Services Facility, paperboard from Covington is processed through extrusion coating, sheeting and custom rewinding operations.

Westvaco has invested more than $400 million in state-of-the-art environmental control equipment and technology at its Alleghany Highlands operations, spends over $30 million annually operating these systems, and has won many awards for its commitment to environmental protection in both its manufacturing and forest management. The driving force for Westvaco's forest management program on nearly 250,000 acres of Virginia woodlands is an ecosystem-based multiple-use management plan that embraces all aspects of forest stewardship, from timber harvesting to endangered species protection.

Since Westvaco's partnership in Virginia began nearly a century ago, the company has continually prospered in the Commonwealth. Today, Westvaco's 3,400 Virginia employees plan for an exciting future as they serve a growing customer base around the world.

health care

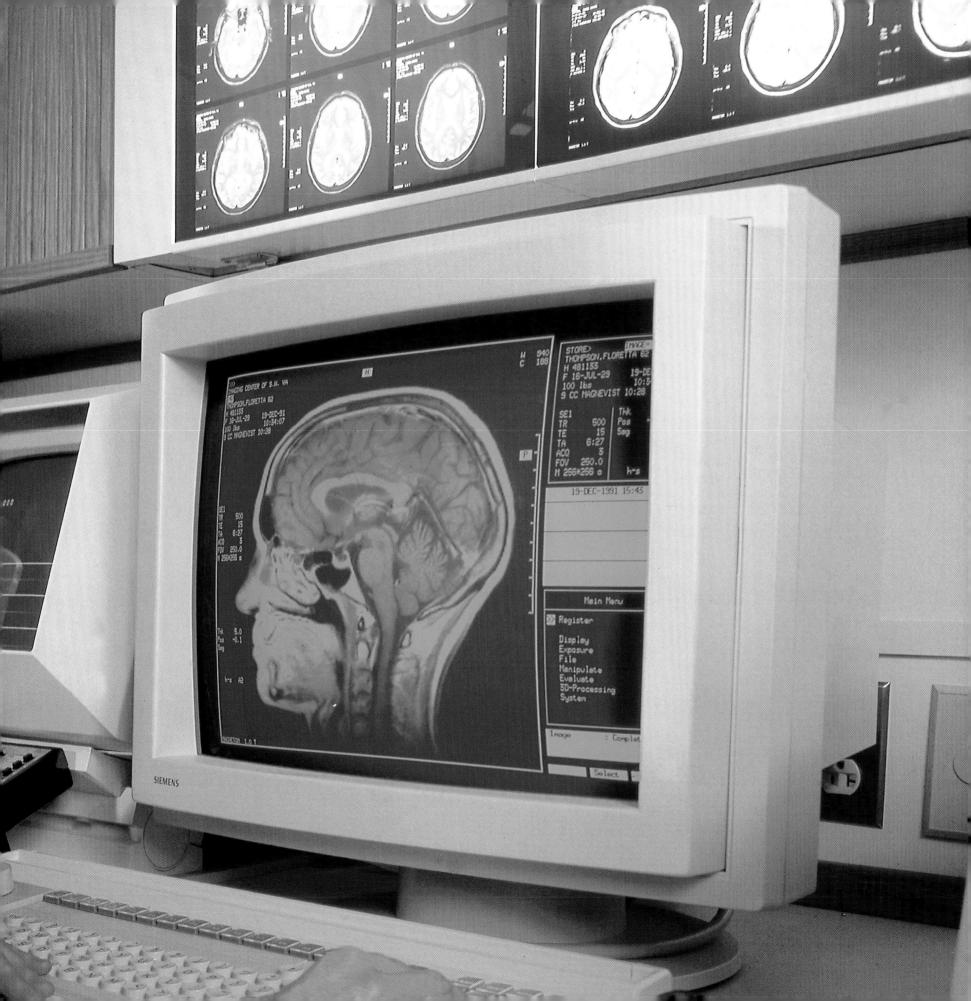

Carilion Health System

It is a name everyone who lives in Western Virginia knows and trusts. It is a business that relies on the human touch of doctors, nurses and other staff members combined with breakthrough advancements in technology and medical services. It is the Region's leading health care provider. With a dozen not-for-profit community-based hospitals and hundreds of primary care providers dedicated to keeping the people of Western Virginia healthy, it is Carilion Health System.

Part of the Region for nearly 100 years, Carilion's roots date back to 1900 when a hospital – now Carilion Roanoke Memorial Hospital – was built at the base of Roanoke's Mill Mountain. While Carilion has grown with the times, its goal remains the same: to improve the health of the communities it serves. And day after day it does just that.

In addition to providing accessible, affordable, high-quality health care to meet the changing needs of the people throughout the Region, Carilion partners with the communities it serves to provide a full scope of wellness, prevention and outreach programs. By joining forces with Roanoke City's health department, public schools and housing authority officials, Carilion's Adolescent Health Partnership program provides health centers for students in area schools. Through Carilion's unique Congregational Nursing program, registered nurses work with churches, synagogues, missions and other related organizations to serve as counselors, educators and liaisons. And through a Community-Based Immunization project, Carilion helps make vaccinations available to all children.

As one of the largest health care providers in Virginia and as Roanoke Valley's largest employer, Carilion also contributes to the economy's wellness. It provides more than 8,000 jobs with an annual payroll of $200 million. It sponsors on-going free clinics, health screenings and educational programs for citizens. It contributes to such community-oriented projects as Habitat for Humanity, and its network of nonprofit hospitals reinvests their surplus dollars in health care needs of the community.

Recognizing that the people of Carilion and its affiliated organizations are the sources of its success, knowledge, skill and compassion, Carilion believes in not only educating community citizens, but in training future physicians. That's why it, in conjunction with the University of Virginia School of Medicine, provides an extensive

Medical Education Program that includes residencies for surgical, family practice, OB/GYN and psychiatry. As a result, Carilion brings the latest medical knowledge into the Region and serves as a major source for providing new physicians.

Carilion also continues meeting and exceeding the changing needs and expectations of approximately one-million people it serves through a variety of personalized care, high-tech and specialized services. For example, Carilion provides the only Level One Trauma Center in western Virginia. Carilion's Cancer Center of Western Virginia – which works in conjunction with the National Cancer Institute, Mayo Clinic and Duke University – is the only location cancer patients in southwest Virginia can access the most advanced treatments.

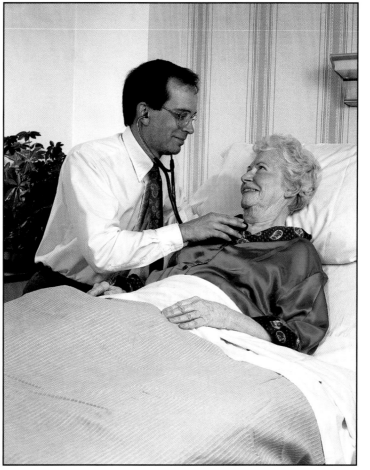

At the same time, the Carilion Medical Center for Children offers specialized care with more than a dozen pediatric specialties, including a Neonatal Intensive Care Unit and a Pediatric Intensive Care Unit. Meanwhile, Carilion Women's Services provides state-of-the-art diagnostic and treatment capabilities such as infertility and reproductive endocrinology care, a Prenatal Diagnostic Center and genetic counseling.

Carilion's nonprofit hospitals include Carilion Roanoke Memorial Hospital, Carilion Roanoke Community Hospital, Carilion Radford Community Hospital, Carilion Saint Albans Hospital in Radford, Burrell Nursing Center in Roanoke, Carilion Giles Memorial Hospital in Pearisburg, Carilion Bedford Memorial Hospital and Carilion Franklin Memorial Hospital in Rocky Mount. It also manages Tazewell Community Hospital, Southside Community Hospital in Farmville, Stonewall Jackson Hospital in Lexington and Wythe County Community Hospital in Wytheville.

As Carilion continues to improve the health of area communities, it will continue to provide accessible, affordable quality health care. In return, the Region's people will continue to look to Carilion to meet their comprehensive health care needs today, tomorrow and for many years to come.

For more information about Carilion Health System, call 540-981-7641 or 1-800-422-8482, or visit www.carilion.com on the World Wide Web.

Lewis-Gale Medical Center

Columbia Lewis-Gale Medical Center – which is recognized as one of the finest health care facilities in the region – has long been a preferred choice for health care in Southwest Virginia. Part of Columbia/HCA Healthcare Corporation, the 521-bed tertiary medical center has provided state-of-the-art medical care for residents of the Roanoke Valley and beyond for nearly 100 years.

Lewis-Gale Medical Center offers more services on one campus than any other facility in the region. Its five centers of excellence include the Regional Heart Center, the Regional Cancer Center, the Regional Rehabilitation Center, the Maternity Care Center and the Center for Behavioral Health.

As part of the world's largest health care provider and one of the region's largest employers, Lewis-Gale is part of a comprehensive health care system that stretches from the Roanoke Valley to the Alleghany Highlands, New River Valley and Richlands. The network, Columbia Healthcare of Southwest Virginia, includes five hospitals – Alleghany Regional Hospital, Clinch Valley Medical Center, Lewis-Gale Medical Center, Montgomery Regional Hospital and Pulaski

Community Hospital –strategically located to serve the region's population and provide sophisticated medical care ranging from open heart surgery to precise computer-controlled radiation therapy and emergency care. Lewis-Gale Medical Center and three of the other hospitals have received the Joint Commission on Accreditation of Healthcare Organizations' highest ranking — Accreditation with Commendation. In fact, Lewis-Gale has received the award for three consecutive surveys — a rare achievement.

In addition to providing comprehensive quality care in a compassionate environment to more than 325,000 patients in Southwest Virginia each year, Columbia Healthcare of Southwest Virginia combines the latest medical technology with a caring and professional staff to meet the changing healthcare needs of a growing community.

Throughout the system, Lewis-Gale operates seven counseling centers staffed with licensed therapists and board-certified psychiatrists to help people deal with the emotional problems which come from living in today's fast-paced world. For convenient access, primary care services are offered in communities throughout Southwest Virginia. Specialized services include accredited inpatient and outpatient rehabilitation centers, featuring the first Easy Street module in Virginia – a rehabilitation component that recreates a real-world environment for therapy; homelike maternity care centers that allow moms to labor, deliver and recuperate in the same room; and cancer care centers with advanced technology that delivers and shapes radiation directly to the tumor site.

Lewis-Gale Clinic, Virginia's largest multi-specialty group practice, and Lewis-Gale Foundation, a nonprofit organization dedicated to providing healthcare education to professionals and citizens throughout the region, are also located on the grounds of the Lewis-Gale Medical Center campus.

While Columbia Healthcare of Southwest Virginia strives to make citizens well, the hospitals also try to keep people healthy. That's why they provide a wide variety of health, wellness and fitness programs such as exercise classes, educational courses, health screenings and business health services throughout the community. The system works with area employers to offer employee assistance programs; extends a unique benefit-filled membership program to people age 50 and

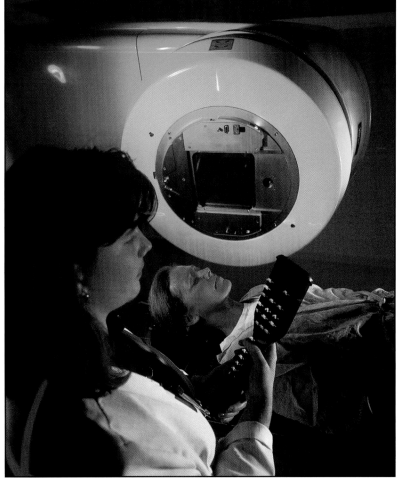

over through Senior Friends; staffs a free, 24-hour Respond line that provides behavioral health assessments, referrals and admissions day or night by phone; and offers a free physician referral and health information service.

With over 3,400 employees, Columbia Healthcare of Southwest Virginia is one of the region's top employers. The five hospitals return more than $22 million dollars to the region's economy each year through tax contributions. In addition to the other hosptials' many donations, Lewis-Gale supports such helping-hand organizations as the United Way, Bradley Free Clinic, Child Health Investment Partnership, American Heart Association, American Cancer Society, the Juvenile Diabetes Foundation, emergency rescue squads and many, many more.

As their long history and outstanding record have proven, Columbia/HCA facilities in Southwest Virginia will continue to provide compassionate, quality care, state-of-the-art medical facilities and highly sophisticated medical technology for many years to come, enhancing the lives of the nearly 500,000 men, women and children who call this region home.

education

College of Health Sciences

The origin of the College of Health Sciences can be traced back to the early 1900s when two hospital-based schools of nursing were founded. Those schools would serve as the foundation for what has become the leading source of health care education for Western Virginia — the College of Health Sciences. As a dedicated partner of the region for nearly 100 years, the College remains steadfast in its commitment to meeting the area's health care education needs.

The College of Health Sciences is one of the state's largest health care education institutions and Southwest Virginia's most comprehensive provider of medical and health care programs. While the original mission of the College was to prepare ethical, knowledgeable, clinically competent and caring health care professionals to provide the highest quality patient care in Western Virginia, graduates can now be found across the United States as well as in other countries.

Accredited by the Commission of Colleges of the Southern Association of Colleges and Schools, the College offers baccalaureate and associate degrees and certificate-level programs to a growing number of students each year. Bachelor's degrees are available in nursing, physician assistant, radiologic sciences, respiratory care, health information administration, science (pre-professional), health

services management and occupational therapy. Associate degrees are offered in emergency health sciences, paramedic, health information technology, nursing, occupational therapy assisting, physical therapy assisting and respiratory therapy. Other degree programs are under development as the College prepares to meet the Region's health care education needs well into the 21st century.

The College launched Virginia's first and much in demand Physician Assistant Program in Fall 1997. Students of the College's charter physician assistant program class are committed to practice in Virginia's medically underserved areas, providing an invaluable service to the rural regions of Virginia. To its credit, 92 percent of College of Health Sciences' graduates pass their licensure examinations on first testing, while 99 percent secure employment within six months of graduation. These statistics suggest quality of program and job market demand.

As it has done for nearly 100 years, the College of Health Sciences will continue to uphold its mission to promote health care education opportunities for career advancement, employment mobility and life-long learning adapted to society's ever-changing medical needs. An asset to Western Virginia, College of Health Sciences' graduates literally save lives for a living.

Hollins University

Since its founding in 1842, Hollins has been a partner in the business, cultural and educational life of the Roanoke Valley. Hollins is the only Roanoke Valley institution offering graduate programs.

Hollins' creative writing program is nationally known for its faculty of published novelists, poets and scholars. According to the *Dictionary of Literary Biography*, it is America's best creative writing program and has graduated some of the best Southern writers, including three Pulitzer Prize winners.

The psychology program is highly respected for its research and speech pathology programs. It led to the founding of the Hollins Communications Research Institute, an internationally-known clinic for stutterers.

The Hollins graduate program in children's literature is the first and only program in America to focus on writing and studying children's literature.

The liberal studies graduate program helps men and women climb the ladder of success with flexible scheduling that respects the demands of home and work. The graduate program in teaching is a flexible year-round program for career teachers who want to learn more about teaching or assume new leadership roles.

The Horizon Program provides a challenging and supportive academic environment for women over the age of 25 who want to return to college and seek a degree. Tailored to the adult student, the program features reentry courses, a dedicated program advisor and a strong support network of Horizon students and alumnae.

The Women's Center helps women plan their lives through non-credit courses, workshops and individual career counseling.

Internships with Roanoke area businesses provide a win-win opportunity for Hollins students and area businesses. In exchange for their labor, students get hands-on work experience and contribute to life in the Valley.

Hollins' campuses in London and Paris and its international programs in Japan, Mexico, Ireland, Austria, Italy, Greece and Jamaica provide important global connections between the campus, the Roanoke Valley and the world.

To learn more about Hollins University, call 540-362-6451, or visit www.hollins.edu. on the web.

Radford University

Nestled among the Blue Ridge Mountains, along the banks of the New River in the City of Radford, Radford University is a comprehensive, coeducational institution committed to serving Southwest Virginians.

It educates more than 8,500 students from the Commonwealth, the country and the world. It offers 112 undergraduate degree and 45 graduate level programs from its 177-acre campus through six colleges: Arts and Sciences, Business and Economics, Education and Human Development, Waldron College of Health and Human Services, Visual and Performing Arts and the Graduate College. It provides one of the lowest tuitions of all four-year, state-supported higher education institutions in Virginia. And it prepares college graduates – more than 93 percent of whom find jobs within three to eight months of graduation – for tomorrow's work force in some of the nation's most prominent occupations such as business, nursing, criminal justice and communications.

Dedicated to meeting the Region's changing educational needs, Radford University offers a variety of undergraduate and graduate degree opportunities in Roanoke by providing courses through the Roanoke Valley Graduate Center, by teaching on-going courses at Virginia Western Community College, and by partnering with Roanoke Memorial Hospital to present nursing programs. At the same time, Radford University's Business Assistance Center offers a broad spectrum of free services and educational

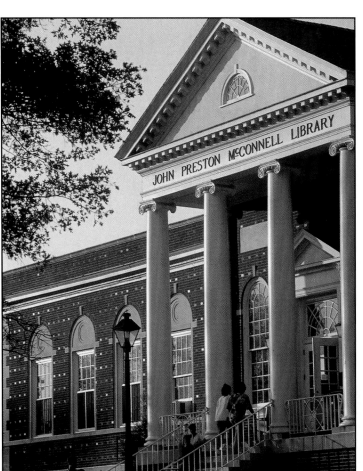

workshops to help area entrepreneurs, small and medium-size companies succeed.

In the cultural arena, Radford University presents a full calendar of activities, including changing art exhibits at the Flossie Martin Art Gallery and nationally-known performers in the areas of dance, theater and music.

Part of the NCAA Division I Big South Conference, the Radford University Highlanders field 20 college athletic teams for men and women, some of whom have gone on to play and coach for America's professional teams. With seven consecutive winning seasons behind the men's basketball team, Radford University's Highlanders hold a record for the longest winning streak among any Virginia Division I school.

Since it opened in 1913, Radford University has served the Commonwealth and the nation through a wide range of academic, cultural, community and research programs. It has educated thousands of mature, responsible, work force ready citizens, and it has continued to meet the changing educational needs of society.

As it prepares for the 21st Century, Radford University will continue to do more of the same.

For more information, contact the Office of Public Relations at 540-831-5182 or visit Radford University's web site at www.runet.edu/

Roanoke College

Ranked among the top ten regional liberal arts colleges in the South by *U.S. News & World Report*, Roanoke College is an integral citizen of the Roanoke Valley, serving the Region in numerous ways.

Established in 1842 and located in Salem, Roanoke College prepares nearly 2,000 students a year for life and citizenship after college, teaching graduates to use their talents to serve the community, society and the world. In fact, some of Roanoke's alumni – 4,000 of whom have remained in the Roanoke Valley and its surrounding areas – have served as members of Congress, sat as Justices of State Supreme Courts, discovered the cause of a devastating disease, led the local Red Cross and managed one of the Region's largest banks. Two Roanoke alumni have even been featured on the cover of *Time Magazine*.

Dedicated to making a difference, Roanoke College's Center for Community Service emphasizes the importance of community service and provides a way for individual students, faculty, staff and campus organizations to get involved. Last year, Roanoke students and personnel gave over 51,000 hours of community service to such programs as Head Start, the Roanoke Area Ministries House for the homeless and the West End Center inner-city outreach program for children, as well as countless others.

Roanoke College also provides an array of cultural opportunities – from theatre performances, changing art exhibits and poetry readings – throughout the year to enrich the lives of students and citizens. In addition, Roanoke's Henry H. Fowler Public Affairs Lecture Series brings such luminaries as former presidents Jimmy Carter and Gerald Ford, former United Nations ambassador Jean Kirkpatrick, Pulitzer Prize-wining columnist Ellen Goodman and author Alex Haley into the Region. Guest lecturers not only speak to students, but also offer free public addresses. And the Kandinksy Trio, the college's artists-in-residence, continue to enhance the Roanoke Valley chamber music scene with their yearly concert series.

Ultimately, as the second oldest Lutheran college in the United States and one of the oldest colleges in Southwest Virginia, Roanoke College serves the educational needs of the Roanoke Valley and beyond.

Not surprisingly, one out of every five students who attend Roanoke is from the Region. But many students – those who are drawn to Roanoke College for its strong academic programs, small town setting, and warm spirit –secure local jobs upon graduation and stay to become lifelong citizens.

Virginia Tech

As Virginia's first land-grant institution, the state's largest and most comprehensive university and one of the nation's top 50 research universities, Virginia Tech is, at the same time, a prominent historic landmark and a leading economic development force.

Located between the Blue Ridge and Allegheny Mountains 35 miles west of Roanoke in Southwestern Virginia, Virginia Tech serves the region, the country and the globe through the discovery, dissemination and application of knowledge.

Each year, Virginia Tech educates approximately 25,000 students from the United States and over 100 countries in nearly 200 nationally-ranked undergraduate and graduate degree programs. Each year, award-winning professors generate a highly-skilled workforce in dozens of fields – from business, science and engineering to education, agriculture and veterinary medicine. Each year, Virginia Tech produces thousands of new alumni who carry on the university's motto Ut Prosim: "That I May Serve."

Graduates and faculty members – from eight colleges located on the 3,000-acre main Blacksburg campus, as well as from the

Roanoke Valley Graduate Center and other locations throughout the state — consistently produce ideas and innovations that help drive today's economy. Meanwhile, more than 60 private-sector companies at the 120-acre Virginia Tech Corporate Research Center are at the forefront of new business applications — some commercializing new technologies from Virginia Tech.

Applying knowledge to real world situations, Virginia Tech reaches out locally and globally. It promotes distance learning, provides educational opportunities to international students and scholars, sponsors professional, leadership and adult education seminars, helps clean the Chesapeake Bay and other state waterways, and helps improve the economic and cultural well being of people throughout the state and around the world.

Since its establishment in 1872, Virginia Tech has upheld its commitment to maintain a balance and synergy between undergraduate and graduate teaching, research and public service programs. For more than 125 years, Virginia Tech has made a difference throughout the Commonwealth, the nation and the world.

quality of life

City of Roanoke

Beneath the Mill Mountain Star, the city's beloved landmark, lies 43 square miles of rolling landscape, eclectic neighborhoods and bustling streets. By mixing the traditions of its past with the strengths of the present and technology of the future, this city, nestled in the heart of the Blue Ridge Mountains, is a major business, financial, and health center.

Roanoke, a five time All-America City, is home to a diverse population of more than 95,000 citizens. It is characterized by safe neighborhoods, myriad recreational opportunities and cultural amenities not usually found in a city this size.

But our quality of life isn't our only asset. Corporations such as First Union, Innotech, Inc., and Norfolk Southern are located here, taking advantage of a highly qualified work force with a work ethic surpassed by none.

It helps that the U.S. Department of Education has recognized some of the city's public schools as among the nation's best. And, as a culturally diverse and growing economic center, citizens' involvement, along with public and private partnerships, has assured Roanoke of being one of the best places to raise a family, according to *Parenting* magazine.

Downtown activity is centered around the historic Farmer's Market, one of the Lyndhurst Foundation's 63 "Great American Places," along with New York's Central Park, Baltimore's Camden Yards and New Orleans' French Quarter. Since 1882, the open-air market has been a popular meeting place, featuring some of the state's best fresh produce and handmade crafts.

Also in downtown is Center in the Square, an educational and cultural center containing museums and a live theater, the Harrison Museum of African American Culture and the Virginia Museum of Transportation. The historic Hotel Roanoke and Conference Center, provides meeting space for conventions and conferences.

It is partnerships fostered between government, business and citizens that provides stability as we tackle the tough issues of the 21st century. Our sense of community and commitment to excellence will ensure our place in Virginia and the nation as the shining "Star City of the South."

For more information about Roanoke, call 540-853-2715, or visit CityWeb at www.ci.roanoke.va.us

Holiday Inn Roanoke Airport

The Holiday Inn Airport is among the finest hotels in the Roanoke Valley and a convenient choice for both business and leisure travelers.

A full service restaurant, Sir Pete's Grille, offers a daily lunch buffet and provides menu items for room service from 6 a.m. to 10 p.m., while Sir Pete's Pub extends an English-style pub and relaxing environment where guests enjoy a variety of international beers, pool, darts, large screen TV and arcade games.

With the completion of a total renovation, the property hosts a number of events for individuals and businesses throughout the Region from wedding receptions to conferences and seminars to the Roanoke Regional Chamber of Commerce's Business After Hours mixers. Event planners can choose from three conference rooms, or a spacious 6,500-square-foot ballroom that can hold up to 600 people, or break into six smaller private spaces, all of which include a telephone with modem jack, individual climate control and adjustable lighting. In addition, The Holiday Inn Airport offers staging capabilities, audio visual equipment and loading dock accessibility.

With 161 sleeping rooms, The Holiday Inn Airport offers a variety of amenities to make guests' stays more enjoyable and productive, including a direct dial phone, oversized work desk, hair dryers, coffee makers, data ports, irons and ironing boards, Nintendo and on-demand movies. For the female traveler, The Holiday Inn Airport can provide rooms with extra security and extra amenities. For business travelers, the hotel offers rooms with recliners. Other hotel features include a Park and Fly rate that enables guests to park their car on the property, receive a night's stay and complimentary transportation to and from the Roanoke Regional Airport. All guests enjoy complete access to a full service health club and discounts to area golf courses, as well as valet service, dry cleaning, bus parking and bell service.

An active community citizen, The Holiday Inn Airport participates in an environmentally-aware conservation program, the Green Program, and hosts such events as the 1997 Juvenile Diabetes Foundation Auction, the Roanoke County Education Advisory Board and sponsors a variety of other local charities.

AmeriSuites

The secret is out ... AmeriSuites is the preferred accommodation for corporate travelers.

AmeriSuites, a wholly-owned subsidiary of Prime Hospitality Corporation based in Fairfield, NJ, – one of the nation's largest hotel management firms which owns AmeriSuites and Wellesley Inns and manages such hotels as Crown Plaza, Marriott and Raddison among others – has established its reputation as America's affordable all-suite hotel.

Specifically designed to meet the needs of business executives and professionals, AmeriSuites' spacious rooms provide guests separate living and sleeping areas fully equipped with everything they need to keep the deals rolling while they're on the road. Such convenient amenities include a refrigerator, wet bar, coffee maker and coffee, an iron and ironing board, a telephone, a modern work desk, a laptop computer dataport, private voice mail message service, and a remote stereo TV/VCR. But if that's not enough, you might consider an upgraded "Taking Care of Business"[SM]

suite. This option buys you a larger, L-shaped desk, two telephone lines, snacks and essential office supplies.

During your stay, AmeriSuites wants to make you feel especially comfortable. That's why it also offers a complimentary deluxe continental breakfast buffet, daily copies of *USA Today*, local phone calls on the house, and free transportation within a three-mile radius. In addition, every Wednesday the hotel sponsors an early evening reception, complete with gratis hors d'oeuvres and beverages.

And while you're away, AmeriSuites makes sure you still have the conveniences of your office and home. A state-of-the-art Business Center stays open 24 hours a day and is furnished with a computer, printer and many of the software applications companies rely on today, as well as a fax machine and copier. A variety of rooms, as well as audio-visual equipment, are available to accommodate your meeting needs and can hold up to 100 people. An indoor swimming pool and exercise room that features stair steppers, treadmills, stationary bicycles and weight machines will help you manage your stress, stay fit and burn off any extra energy. And AmeriSuites even gives you the choice of a self-service laundry facility or door-to-door valet dry-cleaning.

AmeriSuites is conveniently located in such American hot spots as Atlanta, Baltimore, Charlotte, Chicago, Dallas, Miami and Nashville. In Roanoke, AmeriSuites is centrally-located near the Roanoke Regional Airport, Valley View Shopping Mall, Country Side Golf Club, and is within walking distance to a variety of restaurants – from traditional steak and seafood to Italian fare to all-American cuisine. Within minutes of the hotel are such places as Downtown Roanoke, the internationally-acclaimed Center in the Square and the Roanoke Civic Center.

Another benefit of being owned by a leading independent hotel management firm, AmeriSuites offers standard AAA and AARP discounts, reduced weekend rates for leisure travelers, nationally-discounted rates for select firms throughout the nation, and especially attractive prices to local companies who partner with AmeriSuites.

To keep you coming back time and time again, AmeriSuites not only provides you with comfortable accommodations and excellent customer service, but awards frequent travelers who stay at any AmeriSuites hotel 12 nights in a given year with a free, bonus night through its AmeriClub frequent stay program.

So next time you choose AmeriSuites as your place to stay, you can be confident you've made the right choice.

Southeast Rural Community

Water is life. It is necessary for survival because nothing lives without water. But many take this natural resource for granted.

The Southeast Rural Community Assistance Project, formerly known as the Virignia Water Project, is a nonprofit agency committed to helping families experience a quality life by providing safe, affordable and accessible water and wastewater facilities.

Perhaps surprising to many, Virginia ranks second in the country for having the most homes without complete plumbing capabilities. In fact, more than 40,000 homes in the Commonwealth do not have running water, bathrooms, and/or indoor plumbing today. In the Greater Roanoke Region alone there are still more than 5,000 residences that lack complete plumbing facilities.

Since the Southeast Rural Community Assistance Project began in Roanoke in 1970, the numbers have steadily decreased. At that time, there were more than 250,000 households without complete plumbing. Obviously, the Southeast Rural Community Assistance Project is making a difference.

The program began as an attempt to bring safe drinking water to poor rural residents of the Roanoke Valley. As a result of its successes, the project – which was the first of its kind in the country – has grown into a well-respected agency that is part of a network of six technical assistance centers that serve the United States and Puerto Rico.

Based in Roanoke, the Southeast Rural Community Assistance Project's staff and volunteers serve the Region, the Commonwealth of Virginia and six other Southeastern states. They work with rural communities, by providing safe and affordable water and waste water systems; by offering training and technical assistance about related topics; by educating citizens about the importance of clean water and other environmental issues; by funding low interest loans; by working with communities and governments to install new or upgrade water and waste water systems; and by helping facilitate solid waste management to protect the environment.

Governed by a board of directors comprised of public-elected officials, low-income citizens, private and nonprofit agency representatives, the Southeast Rural Community Assistance Project will continue to improve the quality of life for individuals, families and rural communities across the nation.

The Orvis Company, Inc.

Step into any Orvis store and you'll be surrounded by more than a century of sporting tradition. Founded in 1856, Orvis is the nation's oldest mail order company, specializing in fly-fishing and wingshooting gear, custom shotguns, classic country clothing, luggage and travel accessories and gifts for the country home. The Orvis sporting legacy in many ways helped lay the foundation for much of our modern outdoor recreation.

Charles Orvis began making elegant fly-fishing rods for summer visitors from his home in the resort village of Manchester, Vermont. As word spread of the fantastic fly rods coming from Manchester, Orvis realized the incredible opportunity that lay before him and capitalized on it. By the turn of the century, his business savvy and catalog innovation positioned Orvis as a serious mail order force and sales flourished.

Orvis Telemarketing and Distribution Center, Roanoke, VA.

Today, with well over 1,000 employees, Orvis enjoys an international reputation for excellence. Orvis mails 40 million catalogs annually, operates 20 retail stores and supplies over 400 dealers worldwide. The company has major operations in Roanoke, featuring the company's sole distribution center at Roanoke's Centre for Industry and Technology and a full-service retail store along the well-known Market Square.

Orvis is still privately held and family-owned. When Leigh H. Perkins purchased Orvis in 1965, sales were approximately $500,000. Thirty-two years later, sales topped $200 million and continue to grow. In 1990, Orvis purchased the Gokey Company, one of America's manufacturers of fine leather footwear and luggage. And in 1993, Orvis purchased British Fly Reel, makers of the company's popular Clearwater and Battenkill fly-fishing reels.

In keeping with its outdoor heritage, Orvis has pioneered corporate support for environmental conservation, earmarking five percent of pre-tax profits for the protection of fish and wildlife habitat. Nearly $3 million has been raised for conservation in the past decade alone. Projects have ranged widely, from Florida to Alaska, with many local and regional efforts in between. The drive to preserve these habitats is rooted in a company-wide ethic, simply put, that if we are to benefit from the use of our natural resources, we must be willing to act to preserve them.

Index

Corporate Profiles in Excellence Index

BARRY WRIGHT, a Roanoke native, has been in the marketing, publishing and advertising business for over 25 years. Through working on many magazine and book projects he discovered a love for photography. His simple goal is that each image represent Life, Intelligence, Natural Order, and Joy. Besides his photographic endeavors Barry is president of RP Publishing in Salem. He resides in Roanoke County with his wife, Margaret, and their five children.

CHRISTINA M. MACCHERONE, an award-winning writer, public relations specialist and marketing veteran, earned her bachelor's degree in English and Journalism from Virginia Tech. She has served in the marketing department of Radford University, National Business College and Advantage Advertising, Marketing and Design. A winner of nearly 40 awards, her writing has been featured in such regional, national and international publications as *Self Employed Professional, Office Systems Magazine, Virginia Business, The Blue Ridge Business Journal, Cintermex, The Roanoker Magazine, Radford University Magazine* and *Ideas at Work*.

Currently, Ms. Maccherone is president of Serendipity Communications, a firm that provides advertising, marketing, writing, public relations and design services to businesses, non-profit organizations and universities throughout Southwest Virginia. She is vice president of Southwest Virginia's Professional Women Resources and an active member of the National Federation of Press Women, Virginia Press Women, the Roanoke Regional Chamber of Commerce, the Christiansburg-Montgomery County Chamber of Commerce and the Blacksburg Regional Chamber of Commerce. Ms. Maccherone resides in Christiansburg with her husband and daughter.

We wish to thank our families, friends, colleagues and clients for their support which made this project possible. We wish to note that our assignment was to paint a picture – with a broad stroke – of the Greater Roanoke Region, and therefore, recognize that everything that makes the Region what it is could not possibly be included. Finally, we wish you a happy journey as you travel through these pages to discover the beautiful Region we call home.

Barry Wright   Christina Maccherone